ROSCOMMON BEFORE THE FAMINE
The Parishes of Kiltoom and Cam 1749-1845

Maynooth Studies in Local History

GENERAL EDITOR Raymond Gillespie

This pamphlet is one of five new additions to the Maynooth Studies in Local History series in 1996 and adds to an ever growing literature of local history in Ireland. The studies are all drawn from theses submitted as part of the Maynooth M.A. course in local history which began in 1992. Each essay is an exploration not of particular places, usually identified by administrative boundaries, but rather of how in the 'little places' of Ireland their inhabitants lived out their day-to-day lives in the past. As a result the range of subjects covered in these essays is as broad as the experience of any one or even a group of individuals.

Many things bound people together, and drove them apart, in the past and pressures for change came from both within and without regional societies. These bonds and divisions are reflected in these studies: religion at parish level, the comonalities of living in the same town, parish or landed estate, or places where they met each other, such as schools, or fought with each other, as at fairs. It is these complex realities which give the Irish historical experience its richness and diversity and which can only be fully appreciated at the local level and from a series of chronological and geographical perspectives.

These Maynooth Studies in Local History, like the earlier volumes in the series, help us to build more complex pictures of the reality of the Irish past from the middle ages to the present and in doing so presents local history as the vibrant and challenging discipline that it is.

Maynooth Studies in Local History: Number 7

Roscommon Before the Famine

The Parishes of Kiltoom and Cam 1749-1845

William Gacquin

IRISH ACADEMIC PRESS

Set in 10 on 12 point Bembo by
Verbatim Typesetting & Design, Dublin
and published by
IRISH ACADEMIC PRESS LTD
Kill Lane, Blackrock, Co. Dublin, Ireland
and in North America by
IRISH ACADEMIC PRESS LTD
c/o ISBS, 5804 NE Hassalo Street, Portland, OR 97213

A catalogue record for this title
is available from the British Library.

ISBN 0-7165-2597-6

Printed in Ireland
by Colour Books, Dublin

Contents

Preface

I wish to acknowledge the help of a number of people in the preparation of this work. the Directors and staffs of the institutions where research was carried out: the National Archives, the Registry of Deeds, the National Library of Ireland, the Librarian and staff of the library, St Patrick's College, Maynooth; Mrs Helen Kilcline and the staff of Roscommon County Library and Mr Gearoid O'Brien and the staff of Athlone Library. Canon John Greene, parish priest of Kiltoom and Cam for permission to examine the parish register.

I would also like to thank my fellow students in the MA in Local History class 1992-4 at St Patrick's College, Maynooth for their encouragement and insights and in particular to the Course Director Dr Raymond Gillespie for his invaluable guidance.

Finally I would like to thank my wife, Carmel, for her patience, moral support and encouragement.

Introduction

The purpose of this study is to examine a rural community in the century before the Famine. This was a period of relative peace in the country and also a period of rapid population growth. County Roscommon was and is still today one of the most rural counties in the country, which had a population in excess of 250,000 by 1841. The community chosen for this study is the parishes of Kiltoom and Cam, county Roscommon, in the period from 1749 to 1845. These two adjacent parishes were united to form the Roman Catholic parish of Kiltoom and Cam in 1771 when the Revd John Kelly was appointed parish priest of the Union.[1] The parishes were united in the Church of Ireland structure by an Act of Council in 1784.[2] Together these parishes have formed a closeknit community built on the communities of the older parishes and their constituent villages and townlands. It was in this period that many of the parish structures in use today came into existence, for instance structures of church organisation, education and medical care. In the case of the civil parishes which derive from the old medieval parishes Kiltoom is larger than its ecclesiastical counterpart in extent while Cam is smaller but when

Map 1 Location map

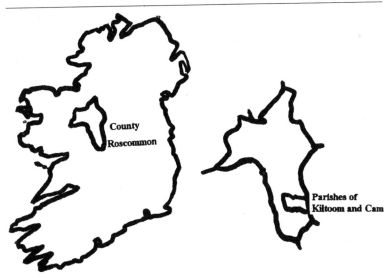

Map 2 Kiltoom and Cam Parish Boundaries

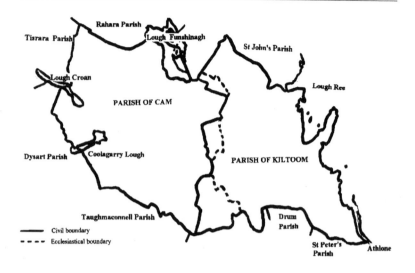

taken together the parishes cover the same area under both civil and ecclesiastical systems (Map 2). This is very helpful as many sources, especially
from the nineteenth century, were collected on the basis of the civil parish.

The parishes are located in the barony of Athlone, county
Roscommon, Ordnance Survey sheets 44-49 and they cover 25,649
statute acres (including some water) subdivided into sixty-four townlands
(Map 3). There is a natural boundary to the east formed by the River
Shannon and Lough Ree. To the north west and south the parishes blend
with the surrounding countryside and at the south east end of the parish is
the town of Athlone, the western part of which was in county
Roscommon during the period under study. The surface of Lough Ree is
125 feet above sea level and this is the lowest point in the parishes. The
land to the east of the Roscommon /Athlone road and much of the south
east of Kiltoom parish lies under 200 feet and it is this area that contains
two areas of bog at Corramore townland and at Knocknanool and
Pollalaher (in Cam parish) townlands. There are three substantial loughs
that lie partly inside Cam parish; Lough Funshinagh is the largest of these
covering over 600 acres of which some 350 acres lie in Cam parish; the
other two are Lough Croan and Coolagarry Lough. All three are tur-
loughs a feature which is common in the central lowland of Ireland where
the base rock of the area is limestone.[3] Lough Funshinagh is one of the
best examples of a turlough in the country. The surface of the water in
these three loughs is approximately 220 feet above sea level, some 100 feet

Map 3 Townlands in Kiltoom and Cam Parishes

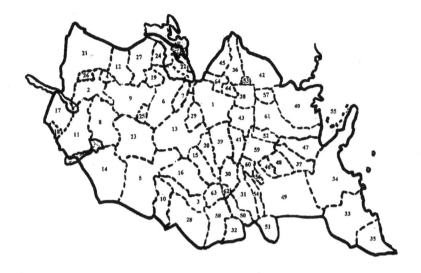

Townlands in the Parishes of Kiltoom and Cam

Parish of Cam (Civil)
1-29

1. Ardmullan	16. Eskerbaun	
2. Ballylion	17. Garrynphort	
3. Brideswell	18. Gortaphuill	
4. Caltraghbeg	19. Gortnasoolboy	
5. Cam	20. Gortnasythe	
6. Carrick	21. Grange	
7. Carrickbeg	22. Inchiroe and	
8. Coolagarry	Gortfree	
9. Coolnageer	23. Kilcar	
10. Cornageeha	24. Kildurney	
11. Cornalee	25. Liscam	
12. Corralea	26. Lismoyle	
13. Curraghboy	27. Lysterfield	
14. Curry	28. Poolalaher	
15. Derryglad	29. Rackans	

Parish of Kiltoom (Civil)
30-64

30. Atteagh	48. Corraclogh
31. Ballycreggan	49. Corramore
32. Ballymullavill	50. Corrantotan
33. Barry Beg	51. Derrynasee
34. Barry More	52. Feamore
35. Bogganfin	53. Flegans
36. Bredagh	54. Gortacoosan
37. Cappalisheen	55. Islands in
38. Carrick	Lough Ree
39. Carrowkeeny	56. Keadagh
40. Carrowmurragh	57. Kiltoom
41. Carrowncloghan	58. Knocknanool
42. Carrownderry	59. Lisbaun
43. Carrownolan	60. Lissygreaghan
44. Carrownure	61. Moyvannan
45. Cartron	62. Mullagh
46. Cloghans Glebe	63. Ratawragh
47. Cornaseer	64. Srahauns

Map 4 Elevation and Loughs in Kiltoom and Cam Parishes

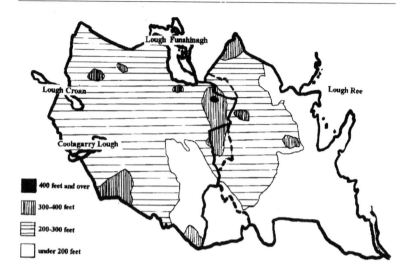

higher than Lough Ree. A large esker starts at the south east corner of Lough Funshinagh and runs southwards through to Knocknanool town-land.[4] This esker is broken by roads leading to Athlone and by the only substantial river in the area, the Cross River running west to east through Cam parish and the southern end of Kiltoom parish to the Shannon. In 1832 this river then called the Granough (probably a misspelling for Crannagh by which it was better known) was described as the largest in the barony of Athlone.[5] Other smaller more broken eskers run in a north-south direction east of the main ridge. Most of Cam parish lies between 200 feet and 300 feet above sea level. It exceeds 300 feet at Cam, Lismoyle, Corralea and at Ardmullan where the highest point in the two parishes is reached at 409 feet (Map 4). ·

The focus of the main roads is Athlone town from where one leads to Roscommon and two others westwards to crossing points on the river Suck at Mount Talbot and Ballyforan. There is a great network of internal roads linking the parishes together. The road leading from Athlone through Brideswell village is shown on the Skinner and Taylor map of 1776.[6]

This is an area of which no study has been carried out for the eigh-teenth or nineteenth century period and this study begins with a survey the parishes as they were in 1749 using the religious census of Elphin dio-cese[7] which gives a snapshot of life in the area for that year and allows for an examination of how the parish community of the mid eighteenth cen-tury worked. The census gives the surnames of the people living in the parishes at that time and the religious adherence of the people is given in most cases. From the census a figure for the population of the parishes is also given, this is very valuable as population figures for county Roscommon are difficult to obtain for the eighteenth century.

These parishes were rural and therefore land and land ownership was always an important issue. The second chapter examines who owned land and what kind of background these owners came from. Some of the different leases and sales which were made over the period 1749 to 1845 will be examined using material principally from the Registry of Deeds. The Registry of Deeds was established in 1708 and had the general aim of copperfastening the Cromwellian and Williamite confiscations and while registration of deeds was not compulsory by the 1750s registration was widespread.[8] It is a very useful source especially for landowning families. A sample of the hundreds of references to places in the parishes of Kiltoom and Cam from 1708 to 1845 covering estates from different areas of the two parishes with owners from different backgrounds will be used.

Chapter three investigates how some of the landlords tried to improve their estates over the century under study. These improvements had benefits for both the landlord himself and also for his tenants. The most adventurous of these improvements was the one which took place at Eskerbaun[9] in the late 1820s. The parishes were assessed for tithes in 1828 and the resulting tithe applotment books[10] give the first opportunity since 1749 to examine the distribution of surnames in the parishes.

In the concluding chapter the changes in society over the period 1749 to 1845 are considered and also the composition of the population by religion. While the Protestant population was small in 1749 it fell further over the period despite their considerable dominance in terms of land ownership. The early nineteenth century saw the development of a formal system of elementary education in Ireland and Kiltoom and Cam parishes were involved with this from the very beginning. These developments and the conditions of the poor within the parishes in the nineteenth century are also considered in this chapter. The Catholic Church became more organised in the parish after 1829 and this led to the building of new churches and the starting of the parish register in 1835.

Griffith's Valuation[11] of 1855 is also examined here as it gives a very detailed breakdown of the number and size of holdings in the parishes. This also gives an opportunity to study the surnames in the parishes just over one hundred years after the religious census of 1749. A comparison of the two lists illustrates a high degree of stability in the population of the parishes over those one hundred and six years. The outbreak of Famine in 1845 has been chosen as a terminal date for this study because of the traumatic effect it had on the local population. The two parishes lost almost one third of their population over the decade 1841 to 1851.

The Eighteenth-Century Community

A detailed picture of the parishes of Kiltoom and Cam in the mid eighteenth century can be drawn from the religious census of the diocese of Elphin of 1749.[1] This census provides valuable information on both parishes for that year. The census data was collected by Edward Synge, the Church of Ireland bishop of Elphin. Dr Synge came to Elphin as bishop in 1740 and remained there until his death in 1762.[2] Some twelve years after the census was taken a letter[3] from Lord Edward Willes to the earl of Warwick says that Bishop Synge was anxious to know the proportion of Protestants to Papists in his diocese. He found from returns made to him by the church wardens (possibly the census itself) that the ratio of Protestants to Papists was three to thirty-nine.[3] The manuscript of the census is deposited in the National Archives, but no details survive of how the census was conducted or precisely who the enumerators were. Using the census of 1749 it will be possible to examine the composition and parochial distribution of population, the religious adherence of the people and the social and occupational structure of the parishes in the mid eighteenth century.

The census gives a figure for the population of the parishes of Kiltoom and Cam in 1749. The total population given is 2,042 of whom forty-eight or 2.35 per cent are Protestants. The census does not indicate how the figure of 2,042 was arrived at as the number of people in each household is not given. However it can be seen from the census that there were 1,047 children and 113 servants in the two parishes giving a total of 1,160 persons. Of the 472 households listed eighteen were occupied by widows and if these are deducted from the total 454 households remain. If these 454 households all had a married couple then 908 persons are to be added to the population as well as the eighteen widows giving a total population of 2,086. This figure is only forty-four greater than the figure given in the census manuscript. This suggests that of the 454 households not occupied by widows forty-four were occupied by either widowers or single men, one of whom is the friar Fr Patrick Conife who lived in Cam parish. The figure of forty-four represents 9.23 per cent of the total number of households, which would not seem unreasonably high as widows alone represent 3.81 per cent of the total households and the forty-four is made up of two categories; widowers and unmarried men. It would therefore seem reasonable to accept the population figure given in the census for the two parishes of 2,042 as being accurate given the limitations of the census itself. Given that there are 472 households this gives a mean of 4.33 persons per household. This multiplier of 4.33 is very similar to a multiplier derived from an estimate of population for Ireland from 1732 which found 4.33 to 4.5 persons per house in the open country and a slightly larger figure in urban areas.[4] A population figure of 2,042 for 1749 gives a density of population of fifty-one persons per square mile. However this population is not distributed evenly over the two parishes.

If the places of abode used in the census are accepted as corresponding to the townlands bearing the same names on the O.S. maps (this may not always be the case) relative population density can be calculated for different areas of the parishes. The number of households in the different areas of the parishes are shown on Map 5 and from these the population density can be calculated for different areas using the multiplier of 4.33 (derived from the census itself above) on each household and the area of each townland from Griffith's Valuation.[5] The areas of lowest population density are Corramore with only three households, giving a population density of 7.2 persons per square mile, and Barrymore with four households and a density of 9.5 persons per square mile. These areas correspond to areas of low elevation with considerable amounts of bog and marginal land. Other areas have higher population density on more fertile land. For example Grange has a population density of ninety-four persons per square mile and Carrick (Cam parish) has a population density of eighty-four persons per square mile. The area of highest population density of 116 persons per square mile is at Moyvannan where there is a mixture of fertile and marginal land. The area of Atteagh on the boundary of the two parishes has a population density close to the mean at 52.5 persons per square mile. The highest area straddling the northern boundary of the two parishes, Ardmullan, with most of its land over 300 feet and reaching a maximun of 409 feet had a population density of 61.8 persons per square mile.

The religious census of Elphin diocese of 1749 is laid out under the following headings;

(a) Parish; the names of the two parishes Kiltoom and Cam are given at the beginning and their boundaries seem to be those used in drawing up the civil parishes later.

(b) Place of abode; forty-four placenames are given under this heading and of these thirty-six are to be found as townland names in the first edition of the Ordnance Survey maps for county Roscommon in 1837. Most of the remaining eight placenames survive to the present day as minor placenames within townlands or in one case as the name of an individual farm, Farneykelly in Carrick townland (Cam parish). There is one place of abode listed in Kiltoom parish the location of which is not certain; Beggarstown. There are also some distinct and substantial townlands

Map 5 Distribution of Households in Kiltoom and Cam Parishes 1749
(Beggarstown not included, location uncertain)

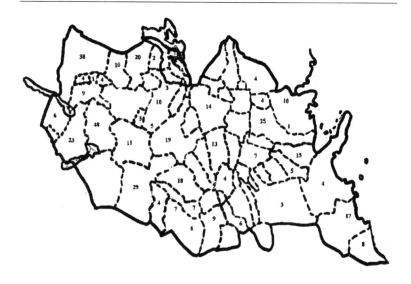

which are missing from the 1749 census. One of these is Coolnageer an
area to which there are many references before and after the time of the
census. It is possible that it was included with Lysterfield as this area or
townland was purchased by Anthony Lyster in 1712 and had previously
been part of Coolnageer.[6] The Lyster family renamed their portion of
Coolnageer as Lysterfield. The places of abode are listed in Table 1.

(c) Head of household; there are 472 households recorded in total for
the two parishes and in all but three cases the surnames are entered clearly.
The spelling of many surnames is different from what they are today and
there are many variations of spelling within the census. It is possible that
one difficulty in recording the surnames was that the majority of the
people used Irish as their everyday language and that the enumerator/s
may not have had much Irish. Irish continued to be used widely in these
parishes for another hundred years and survived in some parts of Cam
parish up to the early twentieth century where the last native speaker was
born in 1865.[7] When surnames which are obviously the same but represented by slight variations in spelling as in the case of *Conife, Coniff,
Coniffe, McConife* or *Naug'n, Naugh'n, Naughten, Naughton* are taken as one
name then there are 175 distinct surnames in the two parishes. These surnames with their frequency are shown in Table 2. The most numerous
names in the parishes were Fallon (twenty-six), Kelly (twenty-six),
Naughten (eighteen), Glinan (eighteen), McDonnell (seventeen), Gately

---

Table 1 Placenames in Kiltoom and Cam Parishes 1749

Religious census of Elphin diocese 1749

Parish of Kiltoom		Parish of Cam	
Bigg Berries	Ardmullan (Part)	Grange	Ard Mullon
Little Berries	Carrowkenny	Lysterfield	Coroughboy
Boginfin	Mivanon	Ballilon	Killcar
Beggarstown	Kiltoom	Lissmoile	Cam
Capalishin	Lisbane	Corelea	Iskerbane
Curramore	Cornasee	Caltraughbeg	Currantober
Attiogh	Milltown Pass	Trine	Polleher
Corromoragh	Corentatan	Lisscom	Corrowduff
Carrowderry	Knocknenool	Carrick	Coolgarry
Newpark		Fereny-Kelly	Cornelee
		Lissflin	Garinford
		Killerny	Cornagee
		Inchroe	

(seventeen) and Dolan (sixteen). The distribution of these surnames in the two parishes is shown on Map 6 and Map 7. Of these seven most numerous names in the parishes in 1749 all but one, Naughten have the majority of their number in Cam parish. For example all the Dolans are in Cam parish as are sixteen of the seventeen Gatelys and half of this family group are in the one area of Coolagarry as is the case with the McDonnell families. All of the most numerous names are the old Gaelic names indigenous to the area and three of them Fallon, Kelly and Naughten were the most numerous names among the landowners in the pre 1641 period as recorded in the Books of Survey and Distribution.[8] There are also in 1749 some new surnames of new landowners of English origin like Lyster, Knight, Hamilton and Stern. All of these were members of the small Protestant community and most lived in Kiltoom parish. The distribution of the Protestant surnames is shown on Map 8, the name of Lucy Davis, a Protestant widow is omitted as she lived in Beggarstown and the location is not certain.

A survey of the male christian names shows that most were saints names. The name John with forty-seven occurrences was the most popular followed by Patrick with thirty-seven, James thirty-five, and Thomas thirty-one. Some old Gaelic first names were still in use; Con(n)or occurred fifteen times Own seven, Art one, Farg's one, Coll one, Murt one and Mans one. With the exception of Connor their frequency was low. In all only ten female christian names were used none with a fre-

Table 2 Surnames and their Frequency in Kiltoom and Cam 1748

Baighelly(2)	Dora(2)	Hay(1)	McGirnna(1)
Banon(2)	Doran(2)	Heal(l)y(2)	McKelly(1)
Bates(2)	Dorcha(1)	He(a)vin(2)	McKina(1)
Beads(1)	Dorehy(1)	Heavy(1)	Mealy(2)
Birn(e)(3)	Dowell(e)(3)	Heneghan(2)	Mears(1)
Bleak(1)	Dowlly(4)	Henry(1)	Mee(1)
Brenan(2)	Doyle(12)	Higgins(3)	Meily(2)
Brooks(1)	Duffy(3)	Hoey(1)	Mellaugh'n(1)
Bryan(1)	Durnan(1)	Hoverty(1)	Menton(1)
Burke(1)	Edwards(1)	Hugh's(3)	Mo(o)rton(1)
Burn(2)	Egan(1)	Judge(1)	Mollaugh(1)
Butler(2)	Erwin(1)	Kearnan(10)	Monogh'n(2)
Cammough(1)	Fallon(26)	Keaughn(1)	Moran(10)
Campbell(1)	Farrell(1)	Keaughane(1)	Morgan(5)
Carroll(1)	Feely(5)	Kein(e)(3)	Morvemough(1)
Cassidy(1)	Feenecan(2)	Keinill(1)	Mulan(e)(7)
Castolo(1)	Fenoughty(2)	Kellelea(1)	Mulchern(1)
Clougher	(1)Fihilly(2)	Kelly(26)	Muldowny(1)
Coffie(2)	Fleming(1)	Ken(n)y(3)	Mulluv'y(3)
Coggall(1)	Flyn(3)	Keough(2)	Mully(1)
Concan'n(1)	Gaffie(3)	Kerelly(1)	Multon(1)
Concarly(1)	Galagher(2)	Kerregan(1)	Murly(4)
Concart(1)	Galvan(4)	Keilty(1)	Murry(4)
(Mc)Conif(f)e(10)	Garmelee(1)	Killbane(1)	Naughten(18)
Connell(1)	Garmly(1)	Killroy(4)	Nevin(1)
Con(n)or(1)	Gately(17)	King(1)	Noon(1)
Conole(1)	Geraghty(3)	Knight(1)	Powdrell(2)
Cooney(2)	Gil(l)igan(7)	Knough(2)	Rock(1)
Corbane(2)	Gill(1)	Leage(3)	Rogers(1)
Corkan(2)	Gillance(1)	Long(1)	Rooney(2)
Cormuck(2)	Glin(2)	Lynch(1)	Rush(1)
Coyle(1)	Glinan(18)	Lyons(3)	Russell(1)
Cravan(4)	Gooan(1)	Lyster(4)	Sheahine(2)
Crickole(2)	Gordan(1)	Maden(1)	Stanton(5)
Cuniham(4)	Gormle(1)	Maloney(1)	Stern(1)
Curelly(1)	Gormuck(10)	Manaughan(1)	Sumough'n(2)
Dalton(1)	Gregan(2)	Manion(5)	Surin(2)
Davis(1)	Grier(1)	Many(1)	Tarp(1)
Daw(1)	Groark(2)	Martin(3)	Terlls(1)
Dillon(1)	Gunane(1)	Mary(1)	Tully(1)
Dolan(16)	Gurhy(2)	McDonnell(17)	Walsh(5)
Donl(l)y(4)	Hamilton(2)	McDonough(1)	Ward(1)
Dooling(1)	Hanroughan(1)	McGea(1)	Watch(2)
Doony(1)	Harny(1)	McGirn(1)	

Map 6 Distribution of Surnames in Kiltoom and Cam Parishes 1749 –
each letter represents one household

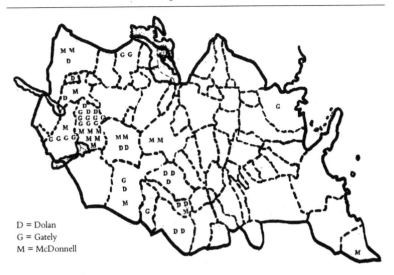

D = Dolan
G = Gately
M = McDonnell

quency greater than one. In the case of the eighteen widows no christian
name is given for ten of them the word 'widow' being used instead.

Among the more unusual surnames were Sumough'n, which occurred
twice, Morvemough and Dorcha. These may be old Gaelic names or the
result of bad translations from Irish as already referred to. The name
Dorcha may be the Irish word dorcha meaning dark and may have been
more descriptive of the person than a proper surname.

(d) Religion; In the case of these two parishes the religion of the head
of the household is given as Papist or Protestant and in the case of fifteen
households this section of the census is left blank. In other parishes for
example Killinvoy those of the Quaker religion are entered as such in the
census. The total number of Protestant households in the two parishes is
twelve and eight of those are in Kiltoom parish. Five of these families
lived in close proximity to each other in the Moyvannan/Newpark area.
There was no Protestant clergyman in either parish. However the Church
of Ireland vestry minutes[9] for the parish of Kiltoom and Cam shows the
Revd William Digby was rector of Kiltoom, Cam and Tisrara from 1718
to 1769. An examination of the 1749 census for the parish of Tisrara
shows that The Revd William Digby was living in Mt. Talbot, county
Roscommon about four miles from the nearest part of Cam parish and
about ten miles from parts of Kiltoom parish. It seems there was no
Protestant church in either parish at this time, the old medieval churches

---

Map 7 Distribution of Surnames in Kiltoom and Cam Parishes 1749 –
each letter represents one household

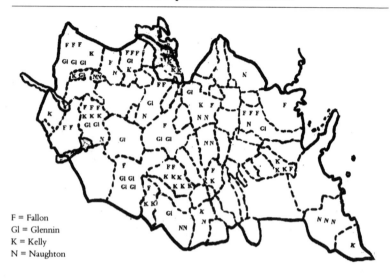

F = Fallon
Gl = Glennin
K = Kelly
N = Naughton

at Cam and Kiltoom having fallen into disrepair. A new church was proposed for Kiltoom and Cam parishes in 1703[10] at Milltownpass but it was never built. A Protestant church was built in Kiltoom parish in 1785 by a gift of £390 from the Board of First Fruits,[11] this church was in fact part of Moyvannan Castle.

The remaining 445 households are all returned as 'Papist', this shows that ninety-six per cent of all the households in both parishes were Catholic. The figure for Catholic households in reality was probably higher as some of those houses for which no return is made regarding religion may have exercised caution when answering questions on religion. For example Hugh Kelly of Lismoyle who is described as a 'gentleman' in the census and probably a landowner may not wish to have shown himself as Catholic. Seven other households for which there is no return regarding religion lived in Moyvannan where as already mentioned there was a concentration of Protestants, they may have seen advantage in remaining silent on the question of religion.

There is only one Catholic priest listed in the census, he was Fr Patrick Conife, a friar who lived at Trien (later part of Ballylion townland). He had two servants in his house, one male and one female. There is an oral tradition[12] that another Friar known locally as 'Padraig-a-Brathair' was ministering in the parish of Cam area at this period. The surname of this second friar was Gately and he had a tombstone erected to the memory of his par-

Map 8 Distribution of Protestant surnames in Kiltoom and Cam Parishes 1749 – each letter reresents one household, Davis not included (location of Beggarstown uncertain)

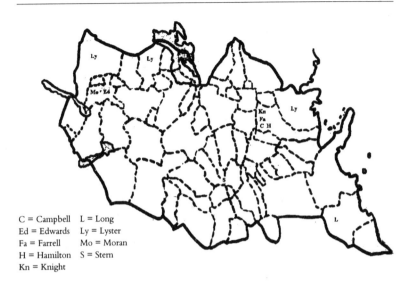

C = Campbell   L = Long
Ed = Edwards   Ly = Lyster
Fa = Farrell   Mo = Moran
H = Hamilton   S = Stern
Kn = Knight

ents in Dysart old cemetery dated 1761, here his name is given as Fr Patrick Gately.[13] There are also two tombstones[14] in Cam old cemetery which give the names of priests from about this period of the eighteenth century, the Revd John Glennon a Carmelite[15] who died on 3 January 1773 and the Revd Marcus Kelly who died on 3 May 1772. The tombstone to the Revd Marcus Kelly was erected by the Revd Laughlin Kelly. These priests may have come from local families or they may have ministered in the locality around the middle of the eighteenth century. Both parishes had masshouses by 1731 and both also had priests.[16] The masshouse for Cam parish was built after 1714 and was located in Curraghboy townland at the western end of the townland. The masshouse or chapel for Kiltoom was probably in Feamore where a chapel was abandoned when a new one was built in Cornaseer townland about 1830. The report of 1731 also mentions that at certain times of the year great crowds gather at St Brigit's well at Brideswell[17] in Cam parish. This parish was dedicated to St Brigit and her pattern day was celebrated on the last Sunday of July, the Pattern probably had its origin in pre christian times.[18] This holy well had achieved some wider attention as testified by the stone plaque erected there in 1625 by Sir Randall McDonnell, the first earl of Antrim.[19]

(e) Profession; this is one of the most interesting parts of the census and it gives a very clear picture of this rural community in the mid eighteenth century. There are returns for 404 of the households on professions, and of the sixty-eight left blank forty are from two adjacent areas of Cornalee and Coolagarry. It may have been the enumerators intention to fill these later. Also in the case of eight households where the head of the house is female the word 'widow' is entered in the professions column. For nine other widows nothing is entered in this column of the census. There are thirty-one separate professions or occupations listed in the census, these are set out in Table 3 and the frequency of each is given.

From Table 3 it can be seen that the greatest number of people with the same profession are those described as labourers. There are 239 labourers in all recorded representing fifty-one per cent of all the households in the parishes. While the census gives no indication how much land was held by each household it would seem likely that those listed as labourers held some land. The large number in this category would seem too great to be required to work on the relatively few large farms in the parishes. Most of the large land-owning households have both male and female servants listed as part of their households. While no leases survive for this group they probably held varying amounts of land sufficient to support their respective households. Some of these labourers may have had no land and earned their living by working on larger farms within the parishes or outside. There are eighteen farmers recorded in the census and some of their leases will be examined in the second chapter. There were also thirty-three tenants and ten cottiers. This latter group all lived at Moyvannan and while all but one of them were Catholic they probably lived on the farms of the three Protestant landowners in that area.

Some of those described as farmers in the census may have owned their own farms. Among the farmers are Bryan Fallon in Coolagarry and Lawrence Fallon in Cornalee these are direct descendants of Redmond O'Fallon, the last elected chief of Clann Uadach[20] (parishes of Cam and Dysart) who died in 1600. The top of the landholding class were those described as 'gentlemen' in the census of whom there are four. Hugh Kelly of Lismoyle, one of those for whom no religion is recorded, the other three were all members of the Lyster family; Thomas Lyster of Grange, another Thomas Lyster in Lysterfield and Anthony Lyster in Newpark (Carrowmurragh townland), all three were Protestants. This family were the descendants of Walter Lister who came to the area about 1600 and is buried in the north east corner of the ruined church at Cam.[21]

The entries in the census under the heading 'profession' cover the full spectrum of society from the gentlemen just described down to the two beggars recorded. There were five ale sellers well dispersed over the two parishes. From Table 3 it can be seen that there was a very self-sufficient community with a large agricultural community served by tailors, weavers, a hatter, wigmakers and feathermongers as well as three millers

Table 3 Occupations in Kiltoom and Cam parishes 1749

Ale-seller	5	Friar	1	Sheriff/Bailiff	1
Beggar	2	Gentleman	4	Smith	7
Carman	26	Hatter	3	Tailor	2
Constable	1	Herd	2	Tenant	33
Cottier	10	Labourer	239	Tilor	1
Cowboy	1	Malster	1	Tinker	1
Dancer	1	Manager	2	Weaver	12
Dealer	1	Mason	1	Widow	8
Farmer	18	Miller	3	Wigmaker	2
Feathermonger	2	Pound-keeper	1	Not given	68
Freeholder	1	Shepherd	12		

and a malster. On the administrative side there was a constable, a sheriff-bailiff and a poundkeeper. There are also some unusual occupations like that of 'dancer'. He may have been a dancing teacher rather than a performer as his household also had one servant. Another unusual occupation is that of one John Murly of Grange who was described as a 'cowboy'. This description may have derived from the Irish expression buachlacht bó or cattle minder which was necessary when cattle were put to summer pastures. Part of Grange townland contains an area of bog and marginal land on its border with Rahara parish and it may have been necessary to take extra care of cattle there during the summer months. One of the most interesting features of the professions listing in the census is the high number of carmen recorded. There were twenty-six with this occupation and they all lived in the parish of Cam. These men were engaged in the transportation of grain, flour and oatmeal to Dublin, the round trip to Dublin took six days.[22] The presence of such a high number of carmen is an indication that corn growing was an important part of the agricultural economy of the parishes of Kiltoom and Cam at that time, and the parishes were in a position to benefit from the bounties offered by the government from the 1750s on to encourage grain production.[23] Ironically it was the goods brought back from Dublin by these carmen which helped to put many of the local tradesmen out of business. Given the number of carmen and the importance of agriculture it is not surprising that there were seven smiths in the two parishes. This fact is also verified by the number of representations of the blacksmiths trade to be found on tombstones in Cam old cemetery.[24] There are six in all and one of these is in memory of Richard Stanton and was erected in 1759[25] and refers to the Richard Stanton listed as a smith in Grange in 1749.

There is only one mason listed in the census which would suggest that there was not much demand for the skills of a mason or perhaps these skills were bought in from outside when needed. The houses of the majority of the people may have been very simple structures possibly with mud walls or a combination of mud with some stone and their construction may have resulted from family or village co-operation. While there are no descriptions of the houses of the poorer classes for the eighteenth century from this area a German traveller passing along the road from Athlone to Ballinasloe (which is less than a mile from parts of Kiltoom parish) in 1806 described the houses he encountered there as 'black mud cabins'.[26] There is no reason to suppose that the houses were of a better quality fifty years earlier. The gentlemen and farmers of the area probably lived in large two storey houses for the most part as was the case with the Lyster houses at Grange and Lysterfield. The Lyster house at Newpark in Kiltoom parish was a three storey house while the house at Lysterfield was described in a family history as being 'liberty hall to the hilt'.[27] The account goes on to say that a pack of hounds were kept there to hunt the south of the county and that between big occasions at the house the natives frequented the house and were welcome there. There is also an account of a wedding of a member of another branch of the Lyster family being held there in 1766.[28]

A poet and farmer from the nearby parish of St John's, Brian Ó Fearghail, in a poem he wrote in Irish in 1786 makes reference to Lysterfield, (which he calls by its Irish name Cul na gCaor) and its occupants[29] giving them Irish names for example James Lyster becomes Shemas Lester. The favourable references in this poem to the Lyster family would seem to suggest that men from Ó Fearghail's cultural background were welcome at Lysterfield House at that time.

(f) Children; the number of children in each household is returned under four subdivisions in the 1749 census. Firstly by religion as either Papist or Protestant and within these divisions as being under or over fourteen. In the case of the house of Anthony Lyster of Newpark, a Protestant gentleman, for example there are three Papist children under fourteen and only one Protestant child under fourteen. This is the only house to have children of both religions recorded. One possible explanation for this is that Anthony Lyster's wife Mary Geoghegan[30] was a Catholic as she came from an old Gaelic family from Castletown-Geoghehan in county Westmeath. When the size of families is examined from the census returns in Table 4 the great majority seventy-nine per cent of the families have between one and three children. The average number of children per family is 2.6. The diaries of another Roscommon man, Charles O'Connor of Ballinagare, tell of severe winters in the early 1740s and of famine in 1744 and 1745[31] all over Ireland and this may help

Table 4 Number of children per family in Kiltoom and Cam 1749

Number of children per family	1	2	3	4	5	6	7	8
Number of families	91	115	112	54	22	7	2	1

Table 5 Number of children per family by profession in Kiltoom and Cam 1749

Profession	Number of families	Number of children per family
Smith	7	3.6
Carman	22	2.9
Farmer	18	2.8
Weaver	10	2.7
Tenant	28	2.6
Shepherd	11	2.6
Ale-Seller	4	2.5
Labourer	210	2.4
Cottier	7	2.0

to explain why such a large number of families had small numbers of children as it is usually children who fall victim of malnutrition and disease in times of famine. When family size is examined under the different occupational classes in Table 5 the group with the highest family size are blacksmiths with 3.6 followed by the carmen with an average family size of 2.9 with farmers in third place with 2.8. These three groups would have worked closely together with the carmen transporting the grain produced by the farmers and the blacksmiths serving the other two groups. The higher than average family size of these groups is probably attributable to the ability of those with larger land holdings to salvage sufficient food even in times of famine to sustain themselves and their families. The largest occupational group, the labourers, had a slightly lower than the average family size but not significantly lower to indicate they suffered more than average families in the parishes during the famine of the years preceding the census.

(g) Servants; the final item in the census refers to servants these like the children are given in four subdivisions by religion and by sex. The total number of servants in Kiltoom and Cam was 113. There were no female Protestant servants and only three male Protestant servants all attached to

Protestant households. The remaining 110 Catholic servants were divided very evenly with fifty-four male and fifty-six female. Of the 472 households fifty-four had at least one servant; these include the households of twenty-four labourers. The single greatest number of servants was eight at the house of Thomas Lyster of Lysterfield. Without any definition of the term servant it is difficult to know if some of those returned under this heading were aged relatives or family friends living in various households.

While there is no mention of education in the census it seems that some form of tuition was available to some families at least about the time of the census. One of the regular priests registered under the terms of the Catholic Relief Act of 1829 was Fr Bartholomew Keelty OP[32] aged seventy-two and then parish priest of Athleague, county Roscommon. He gave his place of birth as Kilderiny, St John's parish but this must be Killerny of Cam parish in the 1749 census where one of those living there was Bar' Kielty, a Catholic farmer, and probably the father of Fr Keelty. He probably received some basic education locally before he joined the Dominican order in Louvain in 1771.[33] Neither does the census give an indication of how the poor were cared for in the mid-eighteenth century. Two beggars are recorded in the census both in Cam parish and both had families. One of these lived in Currantober (now part of Brideswell townland) and an earlier source shows that there was a poor house in Brideswell in 1709 where some poor people were still maintained by the alms of the local Catholics.[34] Some remnant of this system of caring for the poor may have continued into the middle of the eighteenth century.

Land Owners Old and New

As can be seen from the first chapter the parishes of Kiltoom and Cam were a rural community comprising a small number of large estates owned by those described as gentlemen in 1749, together with a number of freeholders and farmers who judging from the size of their households in terms of servants also owned or occupied substantial farms. As well as these two groups there were a large number of labourers and tradesmen who served the needs of the community. This chapter will examine the changes which took place in land ownership and the fortunes of some of the landowners themselves over the following century or so. The main source for the study of these changes is the records in the Registry of Deeds, Henrietta Street, Dublin. The Registry, which was established in 1708 for the protection of purchasers of land had a great variety of material registered there in the early years[1] including leases, marriage agreements, wills and mortgages. This chapter will survey a sample of the transactions involving estates from different parts of Kiltoom and Cam and owners from different backgrounds.

The first group of landowners were settler landlords who had arrived in the parishes before 1700. The most important of these were the Lysters. The Lyster estate at Grange in Cam parish was occupied by Thomas Lyster, a Protestant in 1749 who had seven servants in his household. He was born in 1719 probably in Grange where his father also lived, he was high sheriff of county Roscommon in 1739 and 1745. He married Bridget Fitzgerald and they had five children, he died in 1790.[2] In 1751 a newspaper advertisement[3] stated that the dwelling house and demesne of Grange, 420 acres in all were to be let by Thomas Lyster. This advertisement also stated that the land was divided into parks with iron gates and handsome piers. The lands do not seem to have been let at this time since Anthony Lyster, son of Thomas was listed as a freeholder[4] living at Grange in 1795. Anthony Lyster was killed in 1798 while searching for rebels in county Antrim.[5] A deed memorial of the same year shows Christopher Taffe living at Grange and the lands of Grange forming part of a trust on the marriage of his son George Taffe.[6] In 1752 Thomas Lyster had leased 145 acres one rood, (Irish measure) of the lands of Lower Grange on its boundary with Rahara parish to Peter Sproule of Longfield, Rahara, for three lives renewable forever at a rent of £50 17s. 3d., the renewal fine was one peppercorn.[7] Later in the same year these lands of Lower Grange were put in trust on the marriage of Peter Sproule to Elizabeth Tew[8] of county Meath. This lease was still in operation over hundred years later when the then owners sold their lands through the Landed Estates Court in 1859. When in 1859 other lands in Grange were earning 4s. 7d. per acre in rent the land at Lower Grange was earning only 3s. 5d. per acre under the old lease of 1752 and there was a nominal renewal fine of one peppercorn. The Lyster family severed their connection with Grange in 1803 when the lands were sold[9] to John Farrell, of Eccles St, Dublin, 1,018 acres in all for a total of £8727 12s. 6d. The Lyster house was pulled down[10] but a second house was built which was occupied in 1839 by Patrick Kelly and given a value of £5 in the Valuation Office Field Books.[11]

In the same year as the Grange lands were advertised for letting another Lyster estate at Lysterfield was also advertised for letting for a term of thirty-one years. Lysterfield had been occupied by another Thomas Lyster who had the greatest number of servants of any household in 1749.[12] He died without issue in 1771[13] and by then Lysterfield was rented and occupied by James Lyster of the Newpark branch of the family.[14] The advertisement of 1751 says that the demesne and lands, 230 acres in all, were finely divided into quickset ditches and the meadows had been improved with grass-seed and marl, both water and turbary were convenient and there were two walled gardens at the dwelling house.[15] The descendants of James Lyster continued to live at Lysterfield up to the 1830s and Elizabeth Robinson-Lyster coheir of Thomas Lyster (who died in 1771) married Frederick Trench M.P. who later became Baron Ashtown and she sold Lysterfield to the Trench family.[16]

In 1776 Elizabeth Robinson-Lyster by a deed of mortgage[17] released an undivided moiety of the lands of Lysterfield, Coolnageer, Ardmullan and Gortnasoolboy (and other lands outside Kiltoom and Cam parishes) to the Revd Arthur Champagne for £2,000. The same parcel of lands was mortgaged[18] by the Revd Champagne in 1787 to Francis Hutchinson for £2,000, while the following year in 1788 these lands formed part of a trust set up on the marriage[19] of the Revd Arthur Champagne to Mary Honan. The same lands were the subject of a chancery decree[20] in 1803 where Lord Ashtown and others were plaintiffs and Arthur Champagne and Forbes Champagne, minors were defendants. The bills in the dispute had been lodged in 1797 and the decree divided the lands between the parties. In 1814 these lands were transferred by John Kelly of Balla, county Roscommon who held them by a lease for three lives from Arthur Champagne to James Kelly of Athlone in settlement of a debt.[21] Unlike the Lyster family the Champagne family never lived in Cam parish.

Two of those described as farmers in 1749 were John Knight and John Hamilton of Moyvannan.[22] They held a lease[23] of lands in Lisbaun from the Revd Frederick Trench for three lives at a yearly rent of £43. On the marriage of Godfrey Knight, eldest son of John Knight, in 1757 to Catherine Mitchell of Roscommon, half the interest of John in the leases of Moyvannan, Feamore and Lisbaun were released to Godfrey subject to his paying quarter of the rent to Trench.[24] In a deed dated 1764 an agreement made in January 1760 is recorded whereby James Campbell, one of the freeholders in Moyvannan in 1749 leased the town and lands at Moyvannon to his daughters; Catherine, Elizabeth, Susanna and Francis (Mrs Hamilton) for a rent of £98.[25] James Campbell himself held a lease from the Revd Frederick Trench. In 1815 James and Bartholomew Mulkeran assigned their lease of 77 acres at Feamore to John and James Mulkeran at a rent of £32 14s. 6d., the lessors held a lease from John Knight.[26] Sir Frederick Trench leased some lands in Lisbaun and Corraclogh in 1790 to Edward Kelly[27] with the provision that Kelly could surrender the lease every three years giving six months notice.

A second group were the native Irish families who survived as landlords to the eighteenth century. The lands of Kildurney in Cam parish had been owned by the Keogh family since the sixteenth century[28] and eighty-eight acres of these lands were leased by Mathias Keogh in 1769 to Hugh Kelly of Carrownderry in Kiltoom parish for thirty-one years at a rent of £50 or 11s. 5d. per acre this included arable land as well as loughs and water.[29] Two years later Joan Kelly, sister of Mathias Keogh sold the lands at Kildurney to St George Caulfield of Donamon Castle, county Roscommon.[30] In 1814 the court of chancery ordered that the lands be sold[31] and they were purchased by Philip Duignan of Ballymoe, county Roscommon for £1,600. These lands were some of the earliest to be sold under the Incumbered Estates Act of 1849 when they were purchased in 1852 by Bethal Burton[32] of Dublin, 103 acres one rood and thirty-two perches (statute measure) for £600. The tenant at the time of the sale was Thomas Madden paying a rent of £28. The purchase price in 1852 represents 37.5 per cent of the price paid in 1814 this shows a marked drop in the value of land and the desire of the vendor to make a quick sale.

Another of the old Gaelic families still occupying land and described as farmers in 1749 were the Fallons in Cornalee and Coolagarry. Bryan Fallon held a lease[33] from Henry Kenny of 680 plantation acres of Newtown, Coolagarry for a term of thirty-one years at a rent of £150 since 1747. This lease was replaced by another[34] in 1752 from Elizabeth Kenny to Bryan Fallon, Coolagarry and Lawrence Fallon, Cornalee for the same 680 plantation acres plus sixty-six acres including Cornalee for a term of thirty and a half years and at an increase in rent of £20 to be paid twice a year. Lawrence Fallon put these lands with others in trust on his marriage to Catherine Blake otherwise Sands[35] in consideration of a marriage portion of £600 in 1770. From a newspaper report in *Faulkner's Dublin Journal*[36] dated Sept 1765 Eleanor Fallon wife of Lawrence Fallon of Cornalee died and two years later Lawrence and his nephew William

Fallon conformed to the established church in St Michael's Church, Dublin.[37] This is the only record of converts from the parishes after 1749 although some members of the Lyster family did conform in the earlier part of the eighteenth century.[38] Mrs Fallon's tombstone in Dysart old cemetery gives her date of death as 3 September 1765 in her fifty-sixth year and describes her as a tender parent and most affectionate wife.[39] The only other reference to children of Lawrence Fallon is in 1749 where the census showed he had one child under fourteen.

In 1792 an Act of Parliament was passed[40] to enable Henry Kenny and Elizabeth Dodwell his wife to sell their estates including Cornalee and Coolagarry. In July of 1792 these lands were sold by Anthony and Tredesweda Lee of Wexford town to Robert Blakely[41] of Dublin for £6,060 who sold them in November of the same year to Sir Thomas French[42] of Castlefrench, county Galway for £7,000. A lease[43] of a plot of land in the nearby town of Athlone in 1770 names the lessor as William Fallon of Coolagarry. This is probably the son of Bryan Fallon who obtained the lease of 1747 and in the lease of 1777 one of the lives named is Bryan Fallon son of William. It was this latter Bryan's son Edward who mortgaged[44] a small plot of land he held in Coolagarry from his father for twenty-one years to settle a debt of £13 1s. 5d. with William Dillon a cloth merchant in Athlone in 1811. In 1827 Philip Alley Fallon 'formerly of Coolagarry but now of Brideswell'[45] granted an annuity of £51 4s. to Alicia Keogh and Jesmina Daly out of the lands of Coolagarry until a debt he owed them of £127 13s. 8d. plus interest was paid off. It appears that Philip Alley was a brother of Edward and both sons of Bryan Fallon. This is the last mention of this family in Kiltoom or Cam and the house division of Coolagarry was occupied by James Kelly Esq. in 1828.[46]

In 1823 Gonerville French the youngest son of Sir Thomas French married Clarinda Kenny of Dublin and the lands of Cornalee and Coolagarry were put in trust as part of the marriage settlement.[47] Gonerville French was the owner of these lands when they were put up for sale under the Incumbered Estates Act in 1852.[48] The schedule of the lands for the sale gives a list of the tenants for the two townlands. In Cornalee there were thirty-nine holdings with an average size of 13.4 acres (statute measure), with the largest holding being 47.3 acres and the smallest 0.56 acres. The average rent per acre for the whole townland was 7s. 6d. and the highest rent 10s. per acre was paid by Michael Gately for his 0.56 acres while the lowest rent was 2s. 11d. per acre. All of the leases were held from year to year.

The leases, in the majority of the deeds mentioned, involve large tracts of land often in townland blocks. However there are two examples of leases from Matthew Lyster of Newpark to the occupiers of small holdings. The first of these is a lease[49] made in 1795 for a term of twenty-nine

years of seventy-seven acres arable pasture in Eskerbaun at a rent of £40
to Mathias Fallon, Daniel Fallon, William Watson, Brian Kelly, Frank
Kelly, Pat Kelly and Thomas Gurhy. All of these surnames with the
exception of Watson were in that area in 1749. The following year in
1796 Matthew Lyster leased[50] forty-six acres plantation measure of
Pollalaher for three lives at a rent of £26 to Patrick Power, Patrick Dolan,
John Donnellan, Marc Dolan and Daniel Dolan. All these surnames were
present in the area of Pollalaher in 1749. These tenants were to have 'their
house and fourth sheaf free at the expiration of the lease'. They also had a
right to cut turf in the bog on the townland but this was not a part of the
lease itself. All these lands of Pollalaher, Eskerbaun as well as Newpark,
Carrowmurragh, Corraclogh, Purts, Carrowcloghan, Cappalisheen, and
Brideswell were put into a trust on the marriage of Elizabeth Lyster
daughter of Matthew Lyster and Ralf Smith of Barbaville, county
Westmeath in 1811.[51]

An example of the extensive rights sometimes given to the lessee is to
be found in a lease dated 28 July 1808 from Hugh Kelly of Beagh, county
Roscommon to John Stapelton and his wife Margaret Kelly for the life of
Margaret Kelly of the lands of Lismoyle and Caltraghbeg.[52] Stapelton had
the liberty to pull down the cottages on the lands and to use the materials
as he wished. He remained in occupation of the lands until his death in
1837.[53]

Many of the leases discussed already refer to the letting of land to middlemen and their subletting of the same land to others so that it is often
difficult to ascertain who was the head landlord. One such family of middlemen were the Byrne family who came to Cam parish in the late eighteenth century. Patrick Byrne died in 1790 and was buried in Cam old
cemetery,[54] his son Daniel was involved in leasing land in Cam parish as
were his sons in turn. In 1804 Daniel Byrne had a lease of 265 acres of
Kilcar townland at a rent of £344 from Henry Corr[55] for three lives (all
sons of Daniel Byrne). The rent here at £1 6s. 5d. per acre is much
greater than rents paid in the parish for similar quality land in the eighteenth century and the renewal fine of £100 is much greater than the
peppercorn demanded by Thomas Lyster in 1752. Daniel Byrne died in
1821 and is buried in Cam cemetery where his tombstone[56] describes him
as ' a kind benefactor of the poor'. In 1829 John Byrne son of Daniel surrendered four leases[57] to Lord Clonbrock; one of these was a lease for
twenty-one years to the Revd John Byrne of lands in Curraghboy another
was a lease of 580 acres one rood fifteen perches in Curraghboy and fifty-
eight acres one rood thirty-two perches in Inchiroe and Gortfree townland (except thirty-five acres in the possession of the Revd John Byrne) at
a rent of £651 naming Edward Byrne aged 10 as one of the lives in the
lease which was made in 1808. The final lease was one made in 1829 for

160 acres in Castlesampson, Taughmaconnell parish later used by Lord Clonbrock to resettle some of his tenants from Eskerbaun.[58] While there is no further reference to the Revd John Byrne others of the same surname are mentioned in both the Catholic and Protestant parish registers. A Daniel Byrne, son of Daniel who died in 1821 was a Commissioner[59] for the Tithe Applotment of Cam parish in 1828 and attended Church of Ireland vestry meetings in Kiltoom.[60] Ann Byrne of Curraghboy married George King in Kiltoom church on 18 February 1822.[61] Edward Byrne of Sallowgrove, Coolagarry townland probably the son of Daniel named in the lease surrendered in 1829 had seven children baptised in the Catholic Church at Curraghboy[62] from 1839 to 1852, in many instances the sponsors at these baptisms were Daniel Byrne, Kate Byrne, John King and other close family members.

While the number of landowners was small towards the end of the eighteenth century and while they were almost all Protestant they did show a divergence of opinion when it came to politics as evidenced from a list of county Roscommon freeholders from the 1768-69 period.[63] This shows that eight freeholders; William Fallon, Coolagarry, Stephen Fallon, Milltownpass, John Hamilton, John Knight and Godfrey Knight of Moyvannan, Thomas Lyster, James Lyster and Matthew Lyster of Lysterfield would vote for Mahon as MP while George Brabson, Newpark, James Campbell, Moyvannan, William Fallon, Coolagarry, Thomas Stern, Milltownpass, and Malachy Madden, Curraghboy were to vote for Lord Crofton. Here it can be seen that William Fallon's name is on both lists perhaps, as in matters of religion, he was unsure where his allegiance lay. A later list of freeholders[64] dated 1795-6 from the barony of Athlone lists twenty freeholders from Cam parish and sixteen from Kiltoom parish. These freeholders were mostly occupiers of small holdings and with three exceptions; Anthony Lyster, Grange, Matthew Lyster, Newpark and Peter Sterne, Mullagh, they were all Catholic. The Catholics listed include John Donnellan, Patrick Power, Patrick Dolan and Daniel Dolan, four of the five tenants to whom Matthew Lyster gave a lease of lands in Pollalaher[65] in 1796 and also four members of one family called Beths in Pollalaher, a family with three households in that general area of the parishes in 1749.

Two lists of freeholders from the early nineteenth century show the names of a number of freeholders in the parishes. One list[66] commencing in 1813 shows thirteen freeholds ranging in value from 20s. to 8s. in Cam parish. Only five of those were resident in the parish; John Byrne Esq., Milltown, John Daly, Brideswell, Matt. Lyster, John Moran and Andrew Naughten of Grange. Another freeholder Michael Glennon lived at Carrownderry, Kiltoom and James Fallon of Roscommon had a freehold in Cornalee, he may have been a descendant of Lawrence Fallon who was

Table 6 Landlords in Kiltoom and Cam 1837 (not all townlands included)

Owner	Townlands
Ashtown, Lord	Lysterfield, Pollalaher,Coolnageer
Bern, J.	Kilcar
& Councilar Fallon	
Burne, Esq.	Derryglad
Byrne, Mr	Carrownolan
Champagne, Rev. A.	Ardmullan, Gortnasoolboy
Clonbrock, Lord	Cornageeha, Curraghboy, Eskerbaun, Inchiroe & Gortfree
Digney, Esq. (a minor)	Kildurney
Dillon, Mr	Ballymullavil
Fallon, Mr	Lissygreaghan
Farrell, Mr	Carrowkeeny,Grange, Gortnasythe, Knocknanool
French, Hon. G.	Coolagarry, Cornalee
Grainger, Esq	Liscam, Corrantotan, Ballycreggan, Rathawragh
Hodson, Mr	Barry More, Barry Beg
Kelly, Mr	Atteagh, Derrynasee
Kelly, Capt.	Carrick
Kelly, John	Carrickbeg, Rackans
Kelly, Esq. Ed.	Kiltoom, Carrownderry
Kelly, Esq. Wm.	Garrynphort, Gortaphuill
King, Esq.	Curry
Lloyd, Col.	Bogganfin
Lyster, Mr	Ballylion, Corralea
Smith, H.	Cappalisheen, Carrowmurragh, Carrowcloghan
Smith, Mrs.	Brideswell
St. George, Mr	Cam
Sterns, Mr & Kelly, Mr	Mullagh
Trench, Col. Sir F.	Cartron, Feamore, Keadagh, Lisbaun, Moyvannan, Corraclogh, Cornaseer, Srahauns
Ward, Esq.	Caltraghbeg, Lismoyle

living there up to 1767.[67] A second list of freeholders from the 1836-44 period[68] shows eleven freeholds in Cam and three in Kiltoom ranging in value from 10s. of Elenizor J. Stern's holding at Mullagh to 50s. for most of the others. Half of these fourteen freeholders lived outside the parishes some as far away as Dublin and Kerry.

Table 7 Landlords in Kiltoom and Cam 1852-3

Owner	*Townlands*
Ashtown, Lord	Lysterfield
Bentley	Kilcar
Browne	Brideswell
Burke	Caltraghbeg, Lismoyle
Champagne, A.	Gortnasoolboy, Coolnageer
Clonbrock, Lord	Inchiroe & Gortfree
Dillon	Bredagh, Ardmullan, Ballymullavil
	Carrickbeg, Curraghboy
Duignan	Kildurney
Fallon	Lissygreghan
Farrell	Carrowkeeny, Gortnasythe, Grange,
	Knocknanool
French	Coolagarry,Cornalee
Grainger	Ballycreggan, Mullagh, Carrownolan,
	Corrantotan
Kelly	Corramore, Carrick, Atteagh, Rackans,
	Carrownderry, Shrahauns, Rathawragh,
	Garrynphort, Gortaphuill, Carrownure,
	Kiltoom, Moyvannan
O'Kelly	Derrynasee, Gortacoosan
Lloyd	Barry More, Barry Beg
Lorton, Lord	Eskerbaun, Curry, Cornageeha,
Lyster	Corralea
Smyth	Pollalaher, Carrowcloghan,Carrowmurragh
	Cappalisheen
Talbot	Derryglad
Trench	Keadagh, Cloghans Glebe. Corraclogh,
	Lisbaun, Cornaseer, Feamore, Cartron*
St. George	Cam

* given under French

When the Ordnance Survey name books were being compiled for county Roscommon in 1837 they showed the names of the landowners townland by townland these are set out for Kiltoom and Cam in Table 6. In total twenty-seven landowners are listed some with small holdings like Mr Sterns in Mullagh with twenty-three plantation acres held under a lease from 1809,[69] while Sir Frederick Trench who owned eight townlands in Kiltoom parish comprising almost 1,943 acres was the largest landowner in the parishes. The table is not complete as not all townlands have an owner listed in the name books. There also seem to be some errors as in the case of Kildurney townland where other evidence suggests the owner should be Duignan[70] rather than Digney.

Some fifteen years later one of the MPs for county Roscommon, Fitzstephen French Esq. had a map[71] drawn up showing the landowners of the county in 1852-3. The sources for this map were the documents of the Poor Law Boundary Commissioners. The names of the landowners of Kiltoom and Cam are set out in Table 7. This table gives twenty-one names a reduction from 1837 but this is deceptive as only surnames are entered on the map and a surname such as Kelly, for example, includes a number of individual owners as shown by reference to Table 6. Some new landowners do emerge from Table 7 like Bentley in Kilcar and Burke in Caltraghbeg. This latter owner was Mrs Eliza Burke who inherited the estate from her uncle James P. Ward.[72] There are five new names in 1852-3 while seven of the 1837 names are not recorded on the map.

On the basis of these case studies it seems that there was a considerable turnover of landowners from the mid-eighteenth to the mid-nineteenth century. The older eighteenth-century landlords with their large households like the Lysters at Grange and Lysterfield gave way to new owners who very often did not live on their estates. This was a slow process as in the case of Lysterfield where different branches of the Lysters survived on until the 1830s. This century also saw the last of the old Gaelic families lose their hold on the land; the Keoghs sold Kildurney in 1771 and the Fallons left Coolagarry in the 1820s. Some of the new owners did not put down roots in the area, for example Kildurney changed hands in 1771, 1814 and 1852. This period also saw the growth of the role of the middleman in land transactions, the Byrne family occupied considerable tracts of land in Cam parish from the late eighteenth century onwards. The land became a commodity as in the case of Cornalee and Coolagarry which made a profit of £940 for Robert Blakely of Wexford on his investment of £6,060 from July to November of 1792. Yet other landowning families like the Trenches sometimes occupiers of Moyvannan Castle[73] consolidated their holding of land in Kiltoom parish and acquired some land in Cam parish.

The Improving Landlords

Changes in the ownership of land in the century after 1749 and the decline of some of the old gentry families were paralleled by great changes among the tenantry of the parishes. These changes, especially the increase in the number of tenant families and the ways in which they coped with this increase on a fixed supply of land, will be discussed in this chapter. The first opportunity to examine these changes over the whole area of Kiltoom and Cam comes from the tithe applotment books of 1828.

Both parishes were assessed separately for tithes under the terms of an 1823 Act of Parliament.[1] The applotment for Kiltoom parish[2] was set out by Bernard Cunniffe and Edward Mills Hodson following a Church of Ireland vestry meeting in Kiltoom church[3] in September 1827 at which the Revd Michael Garvey PP attended. The applotment for Cam parish[4] was set out by James Lyster and Daniel Byrne following a special vestry meeting[5] in the Catholic chapel of Curraghboy on 22 October 1827 with James Lyster in the chair. The circumstances of these two vestry meetings suggests that relations were good between the Catholic and Protestant communities in the parishes in those pre-Catholic Emancipation days. From 1735 on only tillage land was titheable in Ireland until 1823 when it was specially provided that pasture land should be made subject to tithe.[6] In Kiltoom and Cam parishes it was decided to levy a fixed rate per acre depending on the quality of the land. In Kiltoom the rates per acre were 10d., 8d., 7.25d. and 6d. while in Cam there were only three rates of 8.25d., 7d. and 5.25d. In all 544 divisions of land were assessed for tithes in both parishes and of these twenty-two per cent were of first class land, fifty-one per cent of second class, twenty-five per cent of third class and two per cent of fourth class, all of the latter group were in Kiltoom.

There are a total of 601 occupiers of the 544 holdings from the tithe applotment books as some divisions of land are held by two or more people. Also some names are entered twice or more in the same area and it is not always possible to be certain if one or more individuals are involved. Accepting those limitations there are 172 distinct surnames set out in Table 8. The frequency of occurrence given in parenthesis. The most numerous names are Dolan (thirty-one), Kelly (twenty-seven), Gately (twenty), Mannion (fifteen). Names which were more dominant in 1749 are Naughten now joint fifth and Fallon now joint seventh. One townland in Cam parish, that of Grange is omitted from the Tithe

Applotment Book. Since this was a densely populated area in 1749 it would if included have influenced the frequency of the various surnames.

The increase in the number of holdings since 1749 and the fact that some holdings are recorded in the names of more than one person in 1828 is evidence that there was a considerable amount of subdivision of the tenants holdings by the early nineteenth century. From the 1841 census returns[7] it can be seen that there are 1,495 houses inhabited in the parishes of Kiltoom and Cam an increase of 1,023 or 216 per cent from the 1749 figure, the distribution of houses and population for 1841 is shown in Map 9. An increase of this magnitude suggests that there must have been subdivision of holdings. An examination of the distribution of the population in 1841 also shows a change from the 1749 situation. Among the most densely populated areas in 1841 are Barrybeg, Barrymore, Boginfin, Cornnaseer and Corramore in Kiltoom parish. These areas were among the least populated in 1749. The density of population from the 1841 census in the various townlands is shown in Map 10. The greatest population density in 1841 is in the small townland of Mullagh equivalent to 1,583 people per square mile, this is based on a small population figure. The areas of highest density in Cam parish are the villages of Brideswell, 442 and Curraghboy (in Carrick townland) 457 people per square mile respectively. The high population in virtually all areas of the parishes raises the question as to how people survived on what was in many cases marginal land. One answer may be provided from the actions of one landlord, Mr Hodson who began to reclaim some of the marginal land on his estate in the late eighteenth century.

The Hodson family were not in Kiltoom parish in 1749 but moved there some time before 1775, when the death in Dublin of the son of Thomas Hodson of Hodson's Bay is recorded.[8] The family came from the neighbouring parish of Saint John's and were descended from Bishop John Hodson[9] of Elphin. Thomas Hodson of Hodson's Bay died in 1797.[10] The Revd Samuel Hodson was a curate in the Church of Ireland parish of Kiltoom from 1800 to 1813[11] and eight of his children were baptised there from 1797 to 1808. In 1821 a deed memorial shows that he lived at Hodson's Bay and leased[12] his lands at Great Berries or Hodson's Bay to his daughter Ann for an annual rent of £310 sterling. The Revd Samuel Hodson died in 1827. Two members of the family lived in the area in 1832 when they were among the signatories to an application for aid for the new National School at Carrick.[13] They were Edward Mill's Hodson probably the son of the Revd Samuel Hodson who was baptised[14] in Kiltoom Church in 1802 and Leonard Hodson.

By 1797 Mr Hodson had begun to improve[15] part of his estate in Barrymore townland which was by then known by the name of Hodson's Bay. The land which Mr Hodson was working on was part of the bog of

Table 8 Surnames and their frequency in Kiltoom and Cam parishes 1828

Banan(1)	Dowd(1)	Keas(2)	Naven(1)
Barrott(1)	Dowling(2)	Keighran(1)	Nealan(2)
Beads(1)	Downey(1)	Kelly(27)	Nolan(2)
Bond(1)	Doyle(12)	Kenny(13)	O'Beirne(1)
Brehany(2)	Duffy(3)	Kerrican(1)	O'Farrell(1)
Brennon(3)	Edwards(1)	Kilcline(1)	O'Reilly(1)
Brien(5)	Fallon(10)	Killeen(1)	Powder(2)
Broderick(1)	Farrell(1)	Kilmartin(2)	Prendergast(1)
Brooks(1)	Feehally(12)	Kilmurry(1)	Quigly(1)
Browne(1)	Feenaghty(3)	Kilroy(4)	Rafferty(1)
Bryan(5)	Finigan(1)	Kine(1)	Ramsey(1)
Burke(3)	Fitzmorris(1)	King(1)	Rattigan(3)
Burns(1)	Gaffy(3)	Knavin(1)	Reddington(4)
Butler(5)	Galagher(9)	Knockee(1)	Reed(1)
Byrne(4)	Galvin(1)	Leech(1)	Rider(1)
Cain(1)	Garvey(1)	Lunneen(3)	Roarke(2)
Carroll(3)	Gately(20)	Lynch(2)	Rowly(1)
Carty(1)	Geevin(1)	Lyons(1)	Runane(1)
Caulfield(3)	Geraghty(5)	Lyster(2)	Seeree(1)
Claffy(1)	Gilday(1)	Mahon(1)	Shanny(2)
Coffey(2)	Gilligan(4)	Mannion(15)	Sharkey(1)
Collins(1)	Glennon(13)	Martin(10)	Shine(4)
Compton(1)	Goodman(1)	McCall(1)	Smyth(2)
Concreigh(1)	Gormley(6)	McDonnell(13)	Stanton(9)
Connelly(1)	Grady(1)	McLoughlin(2)	Stapilton(1)
Conniff(9)	Green(4)	McManus(2)	Sterns(1)
Connolly(2)	Griffin(2)	Mee(4)	Tarmy(1)
Conry(1)	Gurrin(1)	Minchin(1)	Tarpy(1)
Conway(1)	Gurry(3)	Minton(3)	Tims(1)
Corcoran(3)	Hamrock(2)	Mitchell(1)	Tincilint(1)
Corly(2)	Harney(6)	Molin(1)	Tracy(1)
Coyle(3)	Harrington(4)	Monaghan(1)	Tully(1)
Cravin(2)	Healy(1)	Mongan(1)	Tyrrell(2)
Cummins(1)	Heavey(7)	Moran(8)	Waldron(2)
Cunningham(10)	Henaghan(4)	Morgan(1)	Walsh(2)
Curly(3)	Higgins(4)	Morris(1)	Watch(2)
Daly(5)	Hines(1)	Muldoon(1)	White(1)
Darcy(1)	Hodson(2)	Muldowney(1)	
Daw/y(3)	Hore(1)	Mulheran(13)	
Dillon(5)	Hughes(1)	Mullen(6)	
Dougherty(1)	Igo(1)	Mulry(1)	
Dolan(31)	Johnson(1)	Mulvoy(1)	
Don(n)ellon(8)	Judge(1)	Murry(8)	
Donnelly(7)	Keaghron(2)	Mylott(1)	
Doorly(1)	Keaghry(1)	Naghton(13)	

Corramore which lay to the east of the road from Athlone to Roscommon. The drains which had been made by the roadside had made the bog drier and easier to improve on the east side of the road.[16]

The improved bog was divided into roughly rectangular fields of nearly 3.25 Irish acres with discharging drains three feet deep running with the fall eastward towards Lough Ree and crossed with surface drains which were only one foot six inches deep. After the drains were made limestone gravel and stable dung were spread on the bog and a four year crop cycle was begun. Potatoes were sown for the first two years followed by rye which was found to give a better yield than oats or barley. Hay seed was sown with the rye in the third year so that meadow was taken from the reclaimed bog in the fourth year. Over the four years it took to reclaim a piece of bog the cost to Mr Hodson was £38 13s. 10d. per acre[17] while the return from the crops grown over those four years was £60 10s. per acre. This gave a profit of £21 16s. 2d. per acre or £5 9s. profit per acre per year. When the reclamation was completed it was Mr Hodson's intention to set the meadow for three years at £5 or for a longer term of twenty-one years at £1 10s. per acre.[18] The reclamation begun by the Hodson family was still in progress in 1813[19]. It was not the only bog improvement scheme in the area as a tenant farmer named Quigley was paying £3 per acre for reclaimed bog in the Barrymore area on a twenty-one year lease even though he said Mr Hodson's bog was of

---

Map 9 Population and Houses by Townland in Kiltoom and Cam Parishes 1841 (Population/Houses)

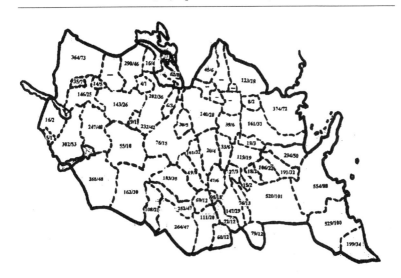

Map 10 Population Density by Townland in Kiltoom and Cam Parishes
1841 (persons per sq. mile)

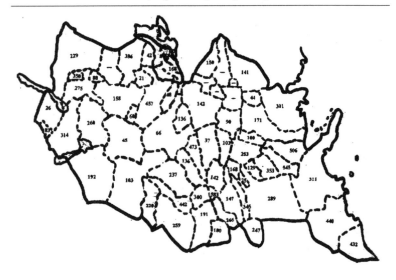

a better quality.[20] In 1749 there were four households in Big Berries
(Barry More) and in 1828 there were five holdings in Barry More including two holdings held by Leonard Hodson Esq. one of a hundred acres
and one of fifty acres.

As well as reclaiming some bog Mr Hodson also started some planting
of trees in the bog about 1800. A number of different varieties of trees
were planted ; scotch fir, larch, spruce fir, birch, alder, oak, ash and Cana-
dian poplar. It was found that the larch and scotch fir did best.[21] Some of
the trees were planted in the furrows as the rotation of crops already outlined progressed. No damage was done to the trees or the crops as all the
work was carried out by spade and there was no ploughing.[22] This shows
that a great quantity of labour was required to carry out the reclamation of
the bog and labour accounted for a large proportion of the cost of the
reclamation work. In the first year labour on the crops alone accounted
for twenty-four per cent of the overall cost, thirty-seven per cent in the
second year and twenty-one per cent in the third year.[23]

Mr Hodson was not untypical in his desire to improve his estate. As
was seen in the second chapter Thomas Lyster of Lysterfield was improving his estate[24] there as early as 1751 by the addition of grass-seed and marl
to the meadows. The motivation here would seem to have been to
increase his income by immediately offering the lands for letting. The
Commissioners appointed to inquire into the bogs of Ireland and the pos-

sibility of draining them reported in 1814 on two areas of bog within the two parishes. The first of these was Corramore bog which lay in the east of Corramore townland and in the western part of Barrymore townland in Kiltoom parish of which Mr Hodson's reclaimed bog formed the eastmost part. This bog was found to be very wet and would require a number of new drains to discharge the water into Lough Ree and the River Shannon.[25] The total estimated cost of the drainage work on this bog was £2,780 12s. 9d.[26] In 1749 only three households were recorded in Corramore but by 1828 there were twenty holdings, twelve of which were held by more than one person,[27] suggesting there may have been as many as thirty-two households in Corramore at that time. By 1841 there were 101 houses with a population of 520 in that townland[28] but by 1855 this had fallen back to sixty-four houses. The western part of this town-land was not part of the bog and it was there that most of the houses were located.

The Commissioners also surveyed Brideswell bog which covered part of Knocknanool and Pollalaher townlands and extended into Taugh-maconnell and Drum parishes. Some drains had already been made in this bog[29] and it was hoped that some few new drains would suffice to drain the bog at an estimated cost of £3,097 6s. 5d. That part of Brideswell bog which lies in Taughmaconnell parish was partly drained as part of a land reclamation[30] for the purpose of resettling tenants between 1824 and 1830.

In the case of Thomas Lyster and Mr Hodson the motivation in get-ting involved in land improvement may have been to increase the income from their estates but there may have been other reasons also. Some land-lords like Lord Clonbrock whose family had owned land in Cam parish from the early seventeenth century[31] may have seen it as part of their role as landlord to look after the interests of their tenants and ensure they could pay their rent. In 1824 the lease on Lord Clonbrock's estate at Eskerbaun came to an end and he decided to tackle the twin problems of overpopulation and subdivision that had arisen on his estate. Prior to 1824 the lands at Eskerbaun had been leased in four lots of seventy-two Irish acres each as shown in the Tithe Applotment Book[32] in 1828 but in reality it was occupied by sixty-two families comprising some 370 individuals.[33] This means that each household had an average of 5.97 people before the resettlement and that the average holding was 4.65 Irish acres some of which was cutaway bogland.[34] The village of Eskerbaun was a very good example of the village system common in Ireland into the nineteenth cen-tury.[35] The land was subdivided according as sons and daughters of the original occupiers married and were given plots on which to build a house and grow sufficient crops to feed themselves.[36] This system was a survival of the rundale system and some families had as little as one fortieth or one

fiftieth part of the original farm leased. This also led to many disputes on
entitlement to various plots of land which became more complex as the
subdivision advanced. These sixty-two families in Eskerbaun had only
thirty cows and eight horses among them.[37] This low number of cows in
particular must have meant shortages of milk from time to time. Since
these tenants lived on the brink of subsistence the landlord could not have
any realistic hopes of increasing his rent income from them.

To tackle this problem Lord Clonbrock selected twenty-seven of the
'most responsible and best conducted' tenants[38] under a new lease and
decided to remove the remaining families from Eskerbaun. Only five families were willing to emigrate and were given assistance of £5 each to go
away.[39] He decided to resettle the other thirty families on another estate of
his at Castlesampson, Taughmaconnell parish, which had previously been
let to a grazier.[40] These tenants were employed and paid wages in the
building of houses for themselves at a cost of £25 16s. 7d. each. They
were allowed to bring their last crops from Eskerbaun and one year's rent
free at Castlesampson.[41] By 1831 these thirty families had forty cows,
twenty-nine sheep, three horses and thirty pigs as well as their corn and
potatoes. The twenty-seven families who remained on in Eskerbaun had
increased their stock of animals to sixteen horses, thirty-five cows and
some heifers; all had a pig and some had two or three pigs.[42] By halving
the number of families in the village they went from having 0.48 cows per
family to having 1.3 cows per family. Fifteen new houses were also built
in Eskerbaun at the expense of the tenants; measuring thirty-four feet by
fourteen feet by nine feet with four rooms in each house. These were
quite substantial houses for tenants in the early nineteenth century. The
timber for the houses was supplied by the landlord[43] from thinnings of
plantations at his demesne of Clonbrock near Ahascragh, county Galway.
At the end of the resettlement there were 162 people in the twenty-seven
families remaining giving an average of six per house. The financial outlay
on the part of the landlord was considerable as can be seen from Table 9
below but the return on the investment was also considerable.

Despite this considerable outlay there was an increase in the rents
which the landlord would receive from £126 to £183 15s. 10d. for
Eskerbaun and from £156 16s. 4d. to £173 5s. 8d. for Castlesampson.
This is an increase of forty-six per cent in the annual rent income from
Eskerbaun which would mean that his investment in Eskerbaun would be
recouped in four years. It took much longer to recoup the investment in
Castlesampson but the landlord had looked after the interests of his tenants
and relieved much hardship and congestion in the village of Eskerbaun.

As well as looking after the interests of his tenants and increasing his
own rent income Lord Clonbrock also hoped that the peace and quiet of
the locality around there would be secured.[44] The rents were usually paid

---

Table 9 Cost of Improvements at Eskerbaun and Castlesampson

Cost of Improvements

Eskerbaun				Castlesampson			
Drain	£113	16s.	0d.	Drain	£135	10s.	2d.
Walls	£67	15s.	5d.	30 houses	£774	18s.	0d.
Allowance to emigrants	£25	0s.	0d.	Rent allowed	£95	7s.	3d.
Townland total	£206	11s.	5d.		£1005	5s.	5d.

Total expenditure £1211   16s.   10d.

---

in cash but at times were charged to the tenants of both Eskerbaun and Castlesampson and paid by labour on the works since their occupancy.[45] The relationship between the landlord and the tenants here seems to have been very good. No attempt was made to coerce the tenants into accepting emigration as the only solution to their problems of overcrowding and there is no evidence that the tenants resisted the dismantling of their old village system. A newspaper report[46] in 1842 records that General Trench gave his annual dinner to his tenants at Moyvannan Castle also indicating a good tenant-landlord relationship. These situations at Eskerbaun and Moyvannan can be contrasted with the rather turbulent relationship between Mrs Sarah Kelly and her tenants at Corramore in 1848 when 20 families were evicted for nonpayment of rent due to the distress caused by the famine.[47]

In the seventy-five years from 1749 to 1824 the number of families in Eskerbaun rose from eighteen to sixty-two and the population increased from seventy-eight (using the multiplier derived from the 1749 census as discussed in the first chapter) to 370. This is an increase of 374 per cent in the population or an annual average increase in population over the seventy-five years of 2.1 per cent per annum. From 1828 to 1841 the number of houses rose by seven and the population went from 162 to 183[48] or an average annual increase of just under one per cent. This slower rate of growth may be the result of more established families remaining on in Eskerbaun and those with younger families going to Castlesampson.

The list of tenants from the time of the resettlement shows that the most numerous surname was Kelly with seven Kelly families remaining on in Eskerbaun and six moving to Castlesampson. Of the seven people named in the lease of 1795 from Matthew Lyster of lands in Eskerbaun three were still living in 1824. They were; Bryan Kelly, Francis Kelly and Daniel Fallon, the latter had moved to Castlesampson. Kelly was also the most numerous surname in 1749 when six of the eighteen households in Eskerbaun had the name Kelly. Also prominent in both places was the name Gurhy which is not to be found in any other part of Kiltoom or Cam parishes in 1749 or 1828, it occurs twice in 1749 and nine times in all in the 1824-28 period. As well as Dolan these are the only surnames to continue in Eskerbaun from 1749 to the 1820s. This suggests that some of the growth in population from 1749 up to the time of the resettlement may have been the result of inward migration to the area of Eskerbaun.

A Time of Change

In the mid-eighteenth century the parishes of Kiltoom and Cam were a largely self-sufficient rural community as can be seen from the analysis of the occupations returned in the census of 1749. There was a relatively low population with a population density of fifty-one people per square mile. Within this community there was a small Protestant population concentrated for the most part in one area of Kiltoom parish. The one hundred years or so after 1749 saw great changes take place most notably in the growth in population and the distribution of that population within the parishes as discussed in the third chapter. More marginal land was brought into cultivation as different landlords made improvements on their estates. The composition of the landlord class within the parishes also changed over this period with the departure of some of the old eighteenth-century landlords and the arrival of new owners many of whom did not live in the parishes. This chapter will examine the parishes in the mid-nineteenth century period and compare and contrast this with the situation in the eighteenth century.

From 1821 onward there is a great deal of information available on population from the census taken every ten years from 1821. Great changes took place in the population of the parishes from 1749 to 1855 as outlined in Table 10.[1]

The 1749 figure is taken from the religious census of Elphin diocese 1749 as discussed in the first chapter. The change from 1749 to 1821 represents a long time span of seventy-two years and no estimates of population are available for the intervening years. The most interesting figure in this table is the average annual increase from 1749 to 1821 of +1.79 per cent. While this is lower than the average annual increase for the following ten year period up to 1831 it is still very high and if it were applied yearly up to 1831 it would give a population for that year of 8,756. The highest population in the parishes of 9,062 is recorded in 1831 but the returns for 1831 are considered to be an over estimate for various reasons.[2] This figure for 1831 would give a population density of 227 people per square mile for the two parishes, four and a half times greater than the population density in 1749. The areas of highest population density in the nineteenth century (see Map 10) were not the same as those of the eighteenth century and some of the reasons for this may be the effect of land reclamation carried out in places like Hodson's Bay in Barrymore town-

Table 10 Population of Kiltoom and Cam parishes 1749-1851			
Year	Population	Percentage change	Average annual percentage change
1749	2,042	–	–
1821	7,332	+259	+1.79
1831	9,062	+23.6	+2.14
1841	7,980	-11.9	-1.26
1851	5,493	-31.2	-3.67

land and surrounding areas which had the highest population density in 1841. From 1831 onwards the population in the parishes was on the decline and there is evidence of emigration from the parish of Kiltoom from as early as 1832.[3] The drop in population from 1841 to 1851 was a result of the effects of the Famine on the area in terms of death and emigration.

The ratio of Catholics to Protestants also changed in the century or so from 1749 on as shown in Table 11. It is necessary to go to the 1861 census returns[4] to get figures for religious affiliation in the mid-nineteenth century. The 1831 figures in this table are taken from the Report of the commission of public instruction.[5]

The figure here for 1749 is taken from the figures given at the end of the census of 1749 and shows a very small Protestant population at that time. The drop in the size of the Protestant population seems to have levelled off by the mid-nineteenth century. While the ratio of Protestants to Catholics is higher in 1861 than in 1831 the number of Protestants in the parishes actually fell from 141 in 1831 to ninety-one in 1861. The significance of these ratios can be seen very clearly by examining (in Table 12) the number of baptisms in the Protestant and Catholic churches of the parishes in the years from 1835 to 1844, these are the first years of the Catholic register and all of 1835 is not covered by the Catholic register. Over this period the number of Protestant baptisms were less than one per cent of the total baptisms within the parishes.

Griffith's Valuation[6] of 1855 gives the names of all the occupiers of land at that time in the two parishes and a description of each tenement as well as the acreage and the valuation of both land and buildings. There were 893 households indicated in the two parishes. However this may be a slight overestimation as it is difficult to know if houses listed as 'Herd's house' in the name of the landlord or immediate lessor were actually occupied. A total of 252 surnames are in these households (see Table 13) of which the most numerous names are; Kelly (forty), Dolan (thirty),

Table 11 Ratio of Catholics to Protestants, Kiltoom and Cam 1749-1861

1749		1831		1861	
Catholic	Protestant	Catholic	Protestant	Catholic	Protestant
97.6	2.4	98.4	1.6	98.1	1.9

Table 12 Baptisms by religion in Kiltoom and Cam, 1835-44

Baptisms	1835	1836	1837	1838	1839	1840	1841	1842	1843	1844
Catholic	67	224	213	253	222	213	216	175	222	175
Protestant	5	2	0	0	2	2	1	4	1	1

Naughten (twenty-four), Doyle (twenty-four), Fallon (eighteen) and McDonnell (seventeen). With the exception of Doyle all these were among the most numerous names recorded in 1749. The other two names which were numerous in 1749, Glennon and Gately, are returned in 1855 as follows Glennon (nine) and Gately (twelve) which indicates that they were still important names in the parishes.

Of the 175 surnames recorded in 1749, eighty-eight or fifty-two per cent of them were still in the parishes in 1855 and four other surnames from 1749 were still in the parishes in 1828 when they were recorded in the tithe applotment books. These figures show a high level of stability in the composition of the population over a century which was at first characterised by rapid growth and then by rapid numerical decline.

Very little can be learned from the Griffith's Valuation on the trades or occupations of the people except that in the description of tenements five forges are mentioned and one individual has the word 'smith' entered after his name. This gives a total of six blacksmiths in the two parishes a reduction of one from the number returned in 1749. The 1841 census shows that there were 184 carmen[7] in county Roscommon. It is difficult to say how many of these might be in Kiltoom or Cam since blacksmiths were required mostly for agricultural work. As can be seen from Table 14 below many of the farms were small and did not require horses to do their work. For example the number of horses in Eskerbaun townland after the resettlement was carried out in 1831 was only sixteen for the twenty-seven families living there.[8]

When the size of the holdings attached to the 893 households is examined as in Table 14 it can be seen that fifty-five per cent of the households had less than ten acres of land and twenty-nine per cent had from ten to twenty acres each. In this rural parish there were 107 households with no

Table 13 Surnames and their frequency in Kiltoom and Cam parishes 1855

Allen(3)	Fahey(1)	Judge(1)	Mulrennan(1)
Armstrong(1)	Fallon(18)	Keaghry(2)	Mulry(1)
Astel(1)	Farrell(4)	Kearney(1)	Mulvy(3)
Beades(6)	Farrington(1)	Keating(1)	Murray(6)
Bannon(3)	Feenarty(2)	Kelly(40)	Mylott(1)
Blaney(1)	Feeny(2)	Kennedy(4)	Naughten(24)
Blithe(1)	Feheely(10)	Kenny(12)	Navin(1)
Bohan(1)	Feneron(3)	Keogh(3)	Nelson(1)
Brennan(2)	Fetherson(1)	Kerrigan(1)	Nolan(2)
Brien(9)	Finigan(3)	Keyes(3)	Noon(1)
Broderick(2)	Fitzgerald(1)	Kilbane(2)	O'Brien(2)
Brookes(1)	Fitzmaurice(3)	Killeen(8)	O'Neill(2)
Brown(4)	Flood(1)	Kilmartin(4)	Parkison(1)
Bryan(2)	Flynn(4)	Kilmurry(2)	Pegnam(1)
Burke(8)	Fogarty(1)	Kilroy(3)	Pierce(2)
Burne(1)	Ford(2)	King(2)	Pim(1)
Burton(1)	Fowley(1)	Kinlin(1)	Power(1)
Butler(9)	Gaffey(3)	Kinneally(1)	Prendergast(1)
Byrne(12)	Gallagher(10)	Leech(2)	Queeney(3)
Carroll(4)	Gannon(10)	Lenihan(3)	Quigley(3)
Caulfield(1)	Gately(12)	Lennon(7)	Quinn(4)
Claffy(2)	Gawkwin(2)	Loftus(1)	Raftery(1)
Clogher(1)	Geraghty(8)	Loughnan(1)	Ramsey(4)
Clooney(1)	Gevron(1)	Lowe(1)	Reddington(2)
Collins(1)	Giblin(1)	Luddeen(1)	Reddy(1)
Comber(2)	Gilligan(2)	Lunneen(11)	Reed(2)
Connaughton(1)	Gleeson(1)	Lynch(5)	Rhattigan(6)
Connolly(7)	Glennon(9)	Lyster(1)	Rickard(1)
Connor(s)(2)	Goodman(3)	M'Cormack (1)	Rooney(3)
Conway(9)	Gordon(2)	M'Dermott(2)	Rourke(7)
Corcoran(8)	Gorman(1)	M'Donnell(17)	Ryan(2)
Corley(1)	Gormly(7)	M'Donagh(1)	Sales(1)
Costello(1)	Granger(2)	M'Gary(1)	Seery(2)
Cottells(1)	Gray(2)	M'Gawley(1)	Shanny(2)
Coy(1)	Green(e)(10)	M'Govern(1)	Shelly(1)
Coyle(12)	Grehan(1)	M'Guire(2)	Sheridan(1)
Coyne(1)	Griffin(2)	M'Keon(3)	Shine(3)
Craven(1)	Gurney(1)	M'Loughlin(3)	Shrahan(1)
Cunniff(e)(8)	Gurry(2)	M'Manus(3)	Shruffin(1)
Cunningham(9)	Hamrock(7)	Madden(2)	Smith(1)

Curley(13)	Hand(3)	Mahon(1)	Smyth(1)
Dalton(1)	Hannon(1)	Malin(2)	St.George(1)
Daly(4)	Harney(2)	Mannion(13)	Staunton(7)
Dea(2)	Harrington(6)	Mara(2)	Stredman(1)
Dignan(3)	Harris(1)	Martin(11)	Strevens(1)
Dillon(4)	Harrison(6)	Mealey(3)	Tarney(1)
Dobbins(2)	Hart(1)	Mee(7)	Tarpey(1)
Dobson(1)	Healy(4)	Menton(2)	Tiernan(1)
Doherty(1)	Heanihan(6)	Miley(2)	Tims(1)
Dolan(30)	Heav(e)y (14)	Mitchell(2)	Tode(1)
Donnellan(9)	Higgins(4)	Molloy(1)	Tracey(1)
Donnelly(10)	Hinton(1)	Monaghan(6)	Trench(1)
Doolan(1)	Hoare(2)	Mongan(1)	Tully(3)
Doorley(1)	Hodson(3)	Moore(1)	Tyrells(1)
Doran(1)	Hogarty(1)	Moran(7)	Waldron(2)
Dowd(2)	Hughes(1)	Morgan(9)	Wall(2)
Downey(3)	Hussey(1)	Morris(6)	Walsh(5)
Doyle(24)	Hynes(6)	Morrison(1)	Ward(3)
Duffy(10)	Jefferson(1)	Muldoon(3)	Watson(1)
Dunnan(2)	Jennings(1)	Mulheran(11)	Wilson(1)
Egan(8)	Jolly(2)	Mullen(4)	
Everage(1)	Jordan(1)	Mullins(9)	

land attached. However a sizable number of these households were in the townlands of Boginfin, Barrybeg and Barrymore which are close to Athlone town where some of the occupants may have worked. But there are some households with no land in almost every townland in both parishes. Of the nineteen per cent with up to five acres of land many had in fact less than one acre. This indicates that there was still a substantial body of agricultural labourers in the parishes after the famine period.

Of the top three per cent of farms with over 100 acres many were the farms of landlords like the 407 acres of demesne lands of Newpark of Henry M. Smythe at Carrowmurragh townland or the 917 acres occupied by Archibald St George in Cam townland.

There are thirty-four landlords listed in Griffith's Valuation (see Table 15) including the Incorporated Society and the Ecclesiastical Commissioners who owned Cam townland and leased it to Archibald St George who then sublet eleven holdings in the townland. In all seven townlands were in dispute and the immediate lessor is shown as the court of Chancery. Among the landlords in 1855 were some whose families were involved in land ownership in the parishes over the previous hun-

	House no land	*House 0-5ac*	*House 5-9ac*	*House 10-19ac*	*Houes 20-49ac*	*House 50-99ac*	*House 100+ac*
Number	107	173	212	256	88	29	28
Per Cent	12	19	24	29	10	3	3

Table 14 Size of holdings in Kiltoom and Cam 1855

dred years; Sir Frederick Trench owned 1833 acres in eight townlands in Kiltoom parish, Arthur Champagne who held three townlands in Cam parish and Henry M. Smythe of Newpark who owned four townlands in all comprising 1883 acres. His mother was Elizabeth Lyster[9] daughter of Matthew Lyster of Newpark. The Honourable Gonervile French owned Coolagarry and Cornalee which his family purchased[10] in 1792. Mrs Sarah Kelly owned five townlands in Kiltoom parish, her late husband's family were one of the old landlord families of the area.[11] Half of the landlords in 1855 were from families that did not have a long association with the parishes of Kiltoom or Cam.

The provision for education up to the 1830s was from private sources but the government had shown a great interest in education from early in the century.[12] The second report of the commissioners of Irish education inquiry shows that there were three schools in Cam parish[13] in 1826; one in Curraghboy operated by Ann Egan in a room fourteen feet square, a second in Corralea operated by Patrick Costello in a barn and a third in Brideswell under Patrick Smith described as a very poor cabin. The income of these teachers ranged from 5s. to 10s. a year paid by the children who were all Roman Catholics. In Kiltoom parish there were five schools.[14] At Moyvannan a school was held in an old house that had been repaired by Col. Trench at a cost of £10. The teacher Winifred Kelly received about 1s. per quarter from the pupils. At Cornaseer under John Connolly there was a school in a stone and lime building, slated with two rooms, and at the Berries (Barrybeg townland) there was another in one room twelve feet square. The teacher was Luke Croghan who got 1s. 8d. to 2s. from the pupils. One Protestant boy read scripture in that school. At Ballymullavil there was a two roomed school under Edmund Kelly. The fifth school had just been established in 1826 in the parish chapel under Edmond Keogh and there were no pupils. Although all the teachers were Catholic three of the schools had Protestant pupils. There were six at Moyvannan, seven at Cornaseer and three at the Berries. While the number of Protestant children attending these schools was small they represented 8.5 per cent of all the pupils at school in Kiltoom parish and 5.4 per cent of all the pupils at school in both parishes. There were no Protestant children in the schools in Cam parish, while the Protestant

population of Kiltoom parish was 2.7 per cent of the total and the
Protestant population of both parishes was only 1.6 per cent of the total.[15]
It would seem that a greater proportion of Protestant parents sent their
children to these 'hedge schools' than did Catholic parents. There were
110 children in these schools in Cam parish and another 188 in Kiltoom
parish, 298 in all of whom sixty-four per cent were male and thirty-six per
cent were female. The only exception to this was at Moyvannan where
there were twenty-eight female pupils out of a total of forty-two, perhaps
this was because the teacher was female. This school at Moyvannon is the
only one recorded in Kiltoom in 1835[16] while there was a national school
in Curraghboy and four other schools in Cam parish. These schools were
operated by Thomas Coleman, Thomas Goffy, Richard Dalton and
Patrick Costello.

There is little evidence of who provided education for those living in
the 'big houses' of the area except for one report from a local newspaper[17]
in 1835. Francis Walsh then principal teacher of the new national school
at Carrick had been engaged to tutor a step-son of James Lyster at
Lysterfield. When he was not paid for his work he sought a decree against
Mr Lyster at Four Roads petty sessions where the Chief Constable Mr
Saparling objected on the grounds that a Catholic teacher had no right to
wages under the law. However the magistrate awarded the decree. A few
weeks later Walsh applied for a levy warrant pursuant to the decree but
the Revd Mr Armstrong (rector of Kiltoom and Cam) one of the magis-
trates refused to grant the warrant. He said that although Walsh was
employed by the board of national education he had no licence to teach as
one had never been given to the Board.

After the announcement by the Chief Secretary Stanley that a national
system of elementary education was to be introduced in Ireland[18] the
parish priest of Kiltoom and Cam the Revd Terrence G. O'Neill immediately applied to the commissioners of national education to build a school
at Carrick[19] in Cam parish and at Ballybay[20] (Cornaseer townland)
Kiltoom parish. These applications give some additional information on
education in the parishes at that time. The application for aid to build the
school at Carrick was made on 7 November 1832 and it held that there
were 11 schools in the two parishes at that time and gave the names of the
teachers; Henry Byrne, Berries, William Lunneen, Fortfield, Mike
Gilligan, Curraghboy, Edmund Kelly, P. Smith, Thomas Staunton, Luke
Croghan, Mike McDonnell, P. Costello and P. M.(rest of surname illegible). The school in Curraghboy was in an old chapel seventy feet by seventeen feet and the schools at Berries and Fortfield both in Kiltoom parish
had been built by Fr O'Neill himself about 1829 but one of them had no
roof. He described all the other schools as mud cabins which is not what
the Inquiry of 1826 had reported seven years earlier. While the Protestant

Table 15 Land owners in Kiltoom and Cam parishes 1855

Owner	*Townlands*
Ashtown, Lord	Lysterfield
Borough, Sir Edward R.	Carrick
Burke, James W.	Caltraghbeg, Lismoyle
Burke, John	Rackans
Burne,Lafford	Bogginfin
Burton, Bethel	Kildurney
Byron, James	Cornageeha, Eskerbaun
Champagne, Rev. A.	Ardmullan, Coolnageer, Gortnasoolboy Lysterfield (part of)
Chancery, Court of	Ballylion, Corralea, Liacam, Barry Beg, Barry More Islands on Lough Ree, Bogginfin (part of)
Dillon, Thomas	Ballymullavill
Dowell, Miss. E.	Cartron
Elliot, Reps. Colonel	Kilcar
Farrell, Reps. Daniel	Grange, Gortnasythe, Carrowkeeny, Knocknanool
French, Hon. G.	Coolagarry, Cornalee
Gannon, J.P.	Lissygreaghan
Granger, William E.	Ballycreggan,Corrantotan, Ratawragh
Hamilton, Amelia	Barry More
Incorporated Society	Gortacoosan
Kelly, Sarah	Carrick (Kiltoom), Carrownderry, Corramore, Kiltoom, Flegans
Kelly, Reps. William	Garrynphort, Gortaphuill
Kilmaine, Lord	Brideswell
King, Rev. Henry	Curry
Lawless, Philip	Carrickbeg
Loughnan, John M.	Atteagh, Mullagh
O'Grady, John	Carrick
O'Kelly, Anthony	Derrynasee
Pim, Thomas jun.	Ardmullan, Srahauns
Smythe, Henry M.	Cappalisheen, Carrowmurragh, Carrowcloghan Pollalaher
Sproule, Diana	Grange (part of)
St, George, Archibald	Cam
Talbot, John	Curraghboy, Derryglad, Inchiroe & Gortfree
Trench, Sir Frederick	Cartron, Cornaeer, Cloghan's Glebe, Corraclogh, Feamore,Keadagh, Lisbaun, Moyvannan
Warde, Charles T.	Bredagh
Wilson, James	Carrownolan

clergy of the parish refused to sign the application Fr O'Neill had no objection to the school being vested in them. Four of the Protestant gentlemen of the parish put their names in agreement to the query sheet about the new school; they were George King, Leonard Hodson, Edward Mills Hodson and Edward D. (rest of surname illegible) as well as twenty-five Catholics including John Byrne of Curraghboy and Eliazor J. Sterne.

The application for aid to build a school at Ballybay (Cornaseer townland) is also dated 1832. Again the Church of Ireland rector did not sign the application but Leonard Hodson and Edward Mills Hodson did sign. From this application it seems that there was a female school in Ballybay at this time conducted by two nuns, Mrs Grace and Mrs Lynch but they probably had left the area by 1839 when salary was granted to Bernard Shanley at the school.[21]

In 1835 application[22] was made to the commissioners of national education to build another school at Cornaseer in the names of Sir Frederick Trench and Leonard Hodson. Fr O'Neill signed the application but said it was not his. This school was not built but an application[23] was made a year later to build a school at Feamore townland with Mr Hodson and Henry Trench as trustees, again the Protestant clergy did not sign the application. This school was opened in 1837 with a Protestant teacher Thomas Shoebottom. He was the only one of the early teachers on whom the inspectors made a favourable report.[24] There were no Protestant children attending this school and in 1839 the new parish priest Fr. John Fitzgerald objected to a Protestant teacher for Catholic children.[25] A solution to the problem was found when the board of national education allowed a monitor to be appointed. The new monitor became the only teacher in the school when Mr Shoebottom retired in late 1839. In 1848 the Revd John Armstrong, rector of Kiltoom and Cam, became manager[26] of the school until his death in 1853 when his son William took over as manager but by 1863 Fr Fitzgerald had become manager of the school.[27]

A fourth school was built in Cam parish in 1835 at Ballintaleva (Cornalee Townland) on the boundary with Dysart parish following an application for aid[28] from the Revd Andrew McGann, parish priest of Dysart and The Honourable Gonervile French the landlord for Cornalee and Coolagarry as well as the neighbouring townlands in Dysart. This was a two storey building costing the commissioners £131 10s. for the building and £93 15s. 4d. for furniture and books[29] while the school at Carrick received a grant of only £50.[30]

From 1834 to 1843 the average attendance at Carrick national school was 112 with the greatest attendance in September 1841 at 187.[31] The average attendance at Ballintaleva school over the same period was 141. The attendance of boys and girls displays the same pattern as was in the private schools of 1826 for example over the period 1834 to 1843 at

Carrick national school the average attendance for boys was seventy-five and that for girls was thirty-five or sixty-seven per cent boys and thirty-three per cent girls of the overall average.[32]

As well as four new national schools two new Catholic churches were also built in the 1830s in the parishes, one at Ballybay (Cornaseer townland) in Kiltoom parish and one at Curraghboy village (Carrick townland). These churches were built[33] by Fr O'Neill who had come to the parish about 1827 as administrator[34] and shows the speed with which advantage was taken of Catholic Emancipation of 1829. When Fr O'Neill died on 2 June 1837 'his untiring and successful efforts for the moral and intellectual improvement of his flock' was recorded in a local newspaper[35] and his death was said to have been regretted by all. Despite these sentiments and his legacy of building in the parish an incident from 1835 shows that not all his flock were appreciative of his efforts. A newspaper report[36] of the 24 November 1835 records a case at Athlone petty sessions where a number of men were accused of assault on Fr O'Neill. A dispute had arisen as a John Gallagher from Kiltoom parish was returning from a fair in Athlone. Gallagher broke free from his attackers and went to Fr O'Neill who having informed the police went with Gallagher back to the scene of the attack. When the dispute started again Fr O'Neill intervened as some of the attackers withdrew about 30 yards and one of them hit Fr O'Neill on the head with a stone. A note[37] written by a later parish priest recording evidence from older people in the parish suggests that this incident caused the death of Fr O'Neill at the relatively early age of forty.

It was not only the Catholic community who were engaged in building at this time but the Church of Ireland also. At a vestry meeting of the parish on 16 May 1836 it was decided to build a new parish church. This new church is marked on the Ordnance Survey map[38] the following year in Cornaseer townland.

Other signs of change in the nineteenth century parish was that central government became involved in the control of law and order. At the time of Fr O'Neill's death in 1837 there were two police barracks[39] in Kiltoom parish one in Kiltoom townland and one beside the new Catholic church and there was also a police barracks in Brideswell,[40] Cam parish. Prior to the establishment of these barracks the Church of Ireland vestry meeting appointed parish constables as in 1800[41] when Michael Doran of Little Berries was parish constable. In 1804[42] Michael Doran was again constable for Kiltoom and Daniel Mulvihill was constable for Cam parish. In 1749 Joe Moran a Protestant living at Ballylion, Cam parish was described as a constable,[43] and there was a pound-keeper and a bailiff in Curraghboy. These are the only references to law and order in 1749 itself. A number of the gentry of the parish served as high sheriff of county Roscommon; Matthew Lyster of Newpark was high sheriff in 1778,[44] James Lyster of

Lysterfield was twice high sheriff in 1799[45] for the second time as was his son James Lyster in 1803 and 1813.[46]

Newspaper reports of crime from the area in the eighteenth century are sporadic, and concern houghing and the maiming of animals in general. In 1778 a meeting in Athlone of the local gentlemen formed an association to bring houghers to justice.[47] Among those listed as victims of these crimes from the Roscommon side of the town were William Fallon and John Burne. In 1779 Bishop James Fallon, Catholic bishop of Elphin asked his priests to condemn the practice of houghing and he warned that those engaged in such crimes were excommunicated forthwith.[48]

One report[49] written by John Burne Esq. of Rockhill (Carrownolan townland) in Kiltoom parish to his brother Godfrey in Dublin in 1812 warned that the country was in a state of rebellion. He went on to say that meetings were being held at night to get herds to give up the animals in their care and he feared his father might lose some of his animals. It appears that his fears were not unfounded as a report in 1826 shows that his father John Burns, a Quaker aged seventy was shot dead in his house in Rockhill and a quantity of arms taken from the house.[50] In 1813 Thomas Beirne, a thresher, was charged with breaking into the house of Michael Feely in Corramore.[51] In May of 1824 a threatening notice was put on the house of a Mr Butler in Cornaseer and signed by 'Captain Rock', this house and another in the area had been attacked by Ribonmen the previous November and two of the attackers were killed by police.[52] This type of crime was still being committed in 1847 when a party of men possibly up to eighteen raided[53] five houses in Cam parish and took guns from the houses of Tully Gallagher, Thomas Mannion, John Fallon and John Dolan. They warned the fifth man William Dea to give up some conacre he held. The police expressed concern that arms were taken.

These were not the only type of crime being committed in the parishes at the time. In 1835 the police reported[54] the murder of a man and the rape of his daughter at Brideswell on their way to Dysart from a fair in Athlone. The mail coach from Athlone to Roscommon was reported robbed several times as in 1800,[55] 1802,[56] and again in 1807.[57]

No evidence survives of the relief of distress among the poor from the eighteenth century with the exception of the poor house in Brideswell in 1709 mentioned in the first chapter. From early in the nineteenth century the Church of Ireland vestry minutes make frequent reference to the provision of money to buy coffins for the burial of paupers. In 1808 the baptism of a foundling named John is recorded[58] and later provision was made by the vestry to pay a nurse to care for him. In 1832 the rector of Kiltoom, the Revd Mr Armstrong was a member[59] of the Board of Health for the Union of Killinvoy set up to deal with an outbreak of cholera.

There was no local board in Kiltoom or Cam but the parish was probably looked after by the Killinvoy Board, a few miles north of Kiltoom or by its counterpart on the west side of Athlone town. There are no records of death from cholera in the parishes but by November 1832 eleven had died of the disease in Athlone[60] and there was frequent contact between both parishes and the town of Athlone.

The report of the commission of inquiry into the poorer classes gives some insight into conditions for the poor in the parishes in 1835. An examination was held by the commission of the Union of Killinvoy and Cam[61] at which John Byrne, Curraghboy and the Revd John Fitzgerald PP, Kiltoom attended among others. It was agreed that while the practice of abandoning children was decreasing the condition of the poorer classes was not good. It was noted also that a labourer or small farmer was unable to save any money and should he die his family would have no means of support. In 1832 the cabins in the vicinity of Athlone on the Roscommon side were described by Issac Weld, who compiled the Statistical Survey of the county, as being among the most wretched to be found in any part of the country but he added that those being built at that time were of a much better quality.[62]

In his reply[63] to queries from the commission the Revd William M'Cleland said there was one deserted child in the parish being cared for by the priest. The Revd Mr M'Cleland said there were eight to ten illegitimate children in both parishes and about forty widows with children in both parishes with no means of support. There were also about forty labourers who left seasonally to seek work mostly in Leinster and some in England. The families of some of these men sometimes went to Leinster but others stayed at home making stockings and flannel to supplement their income. He stated there were about fifty beggars in each parish not all natives to the area who usually received potatoes and free lodgings if they needed it. The Revd Mr M'Cleland seems unsure of many of his answers and uses the word 'about' frequently in his replies. This may be because he was not resident for very long in the area. He officiated at only one baptism[64] in the church in Kiltoom on 24 November 1829 and he may be the William M'Cleland who married[65] Elizabeth Craig in the same church on 14 March 1824.

The parishes of Kiltoom and Cam were served by a dispensary at Brideswell in Cam parish which the commission examined in 1835.[66] The examination was attended by George King who was the governor, secretary and treasurer of the dispensary, also by a smith, a shoemaker, a labourer, the Catholic curate as well as the medical officer. The latter was aged thirty-one and a graduate of Edinburgh who had a private practice in Athlone. He attended the dispensary two days a week. The dispensary was held in a large purpose built one roomed house and had an excellent supply of medicine and furniture. In the previous year the medical officer made 222 house calls from the dispensary and nobody was refused treatment. Difficult cases of lying-in were attended by the medical officer but generally cases were attended by midwives who were said to be grossly ignorant. A meeting of the subscribers to the dispensary was held in July to elect governors and a managing committee. The treasurer was not paid and made reports to the subscribers and the grand jury. In 1833 £71 14s. was collected in subscriptions while medicine cost £42 4s. and the medical officer was paid £80, which was his annual salary.

Some information on the conditions of the community on the eve of the Famine can be obtained from the report of the Devon Commission who took evidence in Athlone from three residents of Cam parish in July 1844 and also from the land agent for one of the landlords. John Donnellan held fifty acres from Mr Champagne at Coolnageer townland.[67] Mr Donnellan had never seen the landlord, his father had taken the land from the father of the then agent. He had no lease but claimed that he and other tenants had been promised leases by the agent and had paid money to obtain leases. He had held a further forty-three acres up to 1841 and when many of his sheep died and he was unable to pay the rent the agent would not let him continue in occupation. Mr Donnellan complained that he had expended £100 on a new house and was not being given any allowance on this expenditure but he did admit that he was a year behind in his rent. Some landlords in the district allowed the tenants to pay rents by bills at an interest charge of from 6d. to 1s. in the pound for three months but not on the estate where Donnellan lived. This evidence on the payment of rents is confirmed by a second witness Edward Byrne[68] of Sallowgrove (Coolagarry townland) who was himself an agent as well as a farmer. The commissioners also took evidence from the agent on Mr Champagne's estate, a Mr Thomas Berry of Hume Street Dublin. Mr Berry[69] said that Donnellan did not spend £100 on his house which was in poor condition, a fact confirmed by the Valuation Office field book[70] which states that Donnellan's house was 'swaggered back and front' and reduced its valuation. Thomas Berry became agent in 1833 and agreed with Donnellan that the landlord had never visited his estate. When Berry got possession of some lands from Pat Donnellan, brother of John, in 1838 he allowed him almost two years rent and allowed Donnellan to collect the £80 conacre rent owed him from those to whom he had sublet.[71] The cost of conacre was very high by 1844 and must have made life very difficult for those who were obliged to take conacre to grow potatoes. Edward Byrne said that conacre was generally costing £5 to £7 per acre and up to £10 per acre in cases. Those who failed to pay their conacre rent on time would have their crop sold to recoup the rent. Mr Byrne gave evidence that when labourers could get work in the Summer they could expect to earn 8*d.* per day, and his name-sake John Byrne of Lysterfield said the rate for a labourer was 6*d.* per day.[72] At a rate of 6*d.* per day a labourer working 300 days a year could expect to earn £7 10*s.* all of which might be used to pay conacre rent to grow potatoes to feed his family.

Mr Berry says he visited the estate at Coolnageer for the first time in 1833 and found the 'habitations quite dark within and full of smoke'.[73] He had a good many chimneys built but some tenants were reluctant to leave the smoke. From 1833 to 1844 he had four new houses built leaving the tenant free to invest his capital in the land itself. He also purchased some clover seed and vetches for the tenants to use and many were employed in drawing stones to masons and making drains which helped them earn money to pay the rent. The rent was previously collected in April and October but he now waited until January for the rent. No receipts were issued but the names were entered in a book in the presence of the two principal tenants. Both Edward Byrne and John Byrne agreed that the tenants usually paid the rent from four to six months after it was due, one gale behind. Edward Byrne said that the rent paid by those with small holdings was usually higher than those who had larger farms.[74] The rent paid by John Donnellan was from 22*s.* to 24*s.* 8*d.* per acre which was fixed in 1824.[75] This is similar to what Edward Byrne said was the average rent for the area at 22*s.* to 23*s.* per acre.[76]

While John Donnellan was more concerned with his own particular problems the other two witnesses gave general information on the area. They both agreed that tillage was the dominant form of farming in the area, while Edward Byrne said that grazing was on the increase. The main crops were potatoes and oats with wheat being grown in some cases. Many of the tillage farms were small, less than ten acres, John Byrne said they were from three to ten acres. Many of these small farms were held in common by poor people who subdivided them, although Edward Byrne said this was being checked. Most small farmers did not have leases which John Byrne says caused them to exhaust the land. The larger farms were held under lease and these farms were being improved. John Byrne who was also a magistrate said there were many good landlords in Ireland and cited as an example Lord Clonbrock who helped his tenants with drainage.[77] This is a reference to the work in Eskerbaun discussed in the third chapter. It was the opinion of Edward Byrne that most tenants held under middlemen rather than head landlords which made it more difficult for them to get leases. Edward Byrne said that the mode usually adopted to recover rent from defaulting tenants was by ejectment. But Thomas Berry in his evidence said that five of the tenants at Coolnageer were a number of years in arrears but no steps had been taken against them because they were 'visited with sickness'. However he did say that one nine acre farm was evicted in 1835 for non payment of rent and the land divided on the adjoining tenants.[78] Edward Byrne and John Byrne agreed that the best managed estates were those on which the landlord was resident.[79]

As with law and order, the provision for relief from poverty was increasingly centralised in the nineteenth century and the parishes were being drawn into a national network. After much debate a poor law system based on the system in operation in England was introduced to Ireland and in 1838 the country was divided into unions.[80] The parishes of Kiltoom and Cam formed part of the Union of Athlone. The effectiveness of this system can be judged by how it responded to the catastrophe of the famine. Initially Kiltoom parish had been united with St John's parish and Cam with Rahara to form local relief committees for the famine but this changed in January 1847 when Kiltoom and Cam parishes were put together to form a local relief committee with Daniel J. Byrne of Lysterfield as chairman.[81] No further evidence is available on the activities of this relief committee.

Both parishes suffered greatly during the Famine period as evidenced by the decline in population from 1841 to 1851 (see Table 10). The decline in population from 7,980 to 5,493 represents a fall of 31.2 per cent over the decade or an average annual decline of 3.67 per cent. This drop in the population of both parishes is much greater than the decline for the country as a whole which was 19.85 per cent but is only slightly higher than that for the barony of Athlone (county Roscommon) which was 30.4 per cent and similar to the decline in county Roscommon as a whole, which lost just over 79,000 people from 1841 to 1851. The drop in population was much greater in civil parish of Cam where the decline was almost forty per cent. The greatest decline was in Lysterfield townland where the population fell from 270 in 1841 to twenty-six in 1851 a ninety per cent decrease and forty of the forty-six houses occupied in 1841 being abandoned.[82] The decimation of the population in this townland also corresponds with the final departure of the Lyster family from the area.[83]

The case of two boys from Grange townland[84] gives an insight into how the poor law system affected the lives of individual families. The two boys, John and James Kelehan, were admitted to the workhouse in Athlone in April 1847 as twins aged eleven. It was discovered in early 1848 that their mother held some land and therefore they were not entitled to relief in the workhouse. They were discharged from the workhouse on 15 February 1848 after breakfast and given some bread and sent home. Both boys were found dead the following morning and an inquiry was ordered by the Poor Law Commissioners. The inquiry was conducted by a Mr Flanagan who called witnesses and ascertained that the boys left the workhouse in good spirits but seemed to delay in the town before starting their journey to Grange about eleven miles away. They were seen by some schoolboys near Feamore school who thought they did not look well, it was then snowing. The two boys warmed themselves in the house of John Gaffey near Curraghboy about 4 p.m. and nobody saw them again until the taller boy arrived at about midnight at the house of Martin Doyle about two miles from Grange. Mr Doyle gave him some bread and allowed him to stay in his barn as the family feared he might have fever and would not let him into the house. He was found dead the following morning as was his brother in a field just west of Curraghboy village. When the local relieving officer visited the boys' mother in Grange he found a house in good repair and about three barrels of wheat in the house and no signs of distress. The boys had an older brother living with their mother. The inquiry found that the boys died of cold and exposure and not from starvation.[84] When asked by the relieving officer why she sent her sons to the workhouse the mother cried and said it was too late to think of that. The boys were not in fact twins as the baptism register of Kiltoom and Cam parish shows; John was baptised on 24 January 1836 and James was baptised on 6 July 1837.[85] This family were no longer living in Grange or any part of Kiltoom or Cam by 1855.[86]

The years from 1749 to 1845 were years of great change. There was a phenomenal growth in the population of the parishes as can be seen from Table 10 which put pressure on the availability of land for the new families. This led to further and further subdivision of holdings and the reclamation of marginal land. The increase in population also caused changes in the social structure of the parishes with more people unable to support themselves, as can be seen from the report of the poor inquiry in 1835. The Catholic church became more organised and centralised and local devotions were suppressed. The Pattern at Brideswell mentioned in 1731[87] seems to have been supressed by the Catholic clergy by the 1830s.[88] According to accounts of the Pattern about that time drinking and dancing went on for several days and nights.[89] New churches were built in both parishes and the clergy became involved with the national schools which they were anxious to establish in the parishes.

As the nineteenth century progressed there was a gradual shift in the balance of influence from the locality to Dublin as the state began to impinge more on the lives of the people. This can be seen first in the provision of a state system of elementary education after 1831. Up to then this was provided for privately and at a local level. By the late 1830s the poor law system had been put in place and played an increasing role in the lives of the people particularly after 1845.

Notes

ABBREVIATIONS

NA   National Archives
NLI   National Library of Ireland
RIA   Royal Irish Academy
RD   Registry of Deeds
IHS   *Irish Historical Studies*

Note: throughout the text the Ordnance Survey spelling of townland names is used except when referring specifically to the Religious census of the diocese of Elphin 1749, particularly in Table 1.

INTRODUCTION

1 Roman Catholic parish register, parish of Kiltoom and Cam, Elphin Diocese, (in local custody)
2 Samuel Lewis, *Topographical dictionary of Ireland*, (2 vols, London, 1837), ii, p. 215
3 J.B. Whittow, *Geology and scenery in Ireland* (London, 1974), pp 134-5.
4 Jeremiah Sheehan, *The eskers of Ireland* (Moate, 1993), p. 9.
5 Issac Weld, *Statistical survey the of county Roscommon* (Dublin, 1832), p. 501.
6 George Taylor and Andrew Skinner, *Maps of the roads of Ireland 1776-1777* (Reprint, Shannon, 1969), p. 77.
7 NA Religious census of Elphin diocese 1749, M 2466
8 John Grenham, *Tracing your Irish ances-tors* (Dublin, 1992), pp 103-14.
9 Thomas Bermingham, *The home colonies of Castlesampson and Iskerbane* (Dublin, 1835), pp 140-54, (copy in RIA, Halliday Pamphlets Vol. 1624(3)).
10 NA Tithe applotment books; Kiltoom parish, Tab 25/52, Cam parish, Tab 25/51.
11 Griffith's Valuation, county Roscommon, barony of Athlone, 1855.

THE EIGHTEENTH CENTURY COMMUNITY

1 NA, Religious census of the diocese of Elphin, M 2466.
2 James Kelly (ed.), *The letters of Lord Chief Baron Edward Willes to the earl of Warwick 1757-1762, an account of Ireland in the mid-eighteenth century,* (Aberystwyth, 1990), p. 134.
3 Kelly, *The letters of Lord Willes 1757-1762,* p. 95.
4 K.H. Connell, *The population of Ireland 1750-1845* (Oxford, 1950), p. 23.
5 Griffith's Valuation, County Roscommon, Barony of Athlone, 1855.
6 RD Deed Number 9-56-3236.
7 NA, 1901 Census Returns, County Roscommon, Cam parish, Cornalee townland.
8 R.C. Simington, *Books of survey and distribution, vol. 1, County Roscommon* (Dublin, 1949), pp 96-102.
9 Church of Ireland Vestry Minutes, Kiltoom Parish, Typescript copy, Burgess Papers, Athlone Library, p. ii.
10 J.C. Erck, *Ecclesiastical Register*, vol 1, p. 241.
11 Samuel Lewis, *Topographical Dictionary of Ireland,* (2 vols., London, 1837), ii, p. 215.

12 Related to me by the late John J. Gately, Castletown, Curraghboy, County Roscommon.
13 Genealogical Office, Dublin, Tombstone Inscriptions Dysart old cemetery, I.G.R.S. Collection 103.
14 William Gacquin, *Tombstone Inscriptions Cam old cemetery* (1992), pp. 11-12
15 Peter O'Dwyer, *The Irish Carmelites* (Dublin, 1988), p. 153.
16 'Report on the state of popery in Ireland 1731', in *Archivium Hibernicum*, iii (1914), p. 140.
17 'Report on the state of Popery in Ireland 1731', in *Archivium Hibernicum*, iii (1914) p. 140.
18 Maire MacNeill, *The festival of Lughnasa* (London, 1962), pp. 633-4.
19 Stone plaque on wall of ruined chapel at Brideswell, county Roscommon.
20 Timothy Cronin, 'The foundations of landlordism in the barony of Athlone 1566-1666' (M.A. Thesis UCG, 1977), pp. 191-2.
21 Rev. H.L. Lyster-Denny, *Memorial of an ancient house* (Edinburgh, 1913), p. 20.
22 Timothy Cronin, *History of Roscommon 1566- notes on* (Department of Education, 1976) unpublished, available in Dept. of Education, Marlboro Street, Dublin
23 R.F. Foster, *Modern Ireland 1600-1972* (London, 1988), p. 199.
24 William Gacquin, *Tombstone Inscriptions Cam old cemetery* (1992), pp. 39-42.
25 William Gacquin, *Tombstone Inscriptions Cam old cemetery* (1992), p. 22.
26 C.J. Woods, 'J.F. Hering's description of Connacht' in *IHS* xxv, no. 99 (May 1987), p. 316.
27 Lyster-Denny, *Memorial*, p. 25.
28 Lyster-Denny, *Memorial*, p. 62.
29 RIA, Ms. 23 E 7.
30 Lyster-Denny, *Memorial*, p. 23.
31 Printed in *Galvia* i (1954), p. 38.
32 'A list of regulars reistered in Ireland', in *Archivium Hibernicum*, iii (1914), p. 78.
33 Luke Taheny O.P., *The Dominicans of Roscommon* (Dublin, n.d.), p. 51.
34 Thomas Molyneux, 'Journey to Connaught 1709', in *Miscellany of the Irish Archaelogical Society, vol. 1* (Dublin, 1846) p. 161.

LAND OWNERS OLD AND NEW

1 Peter Roebuck, 'The Irish Registry of Deeds; a comparative study' in *IHS*, xviii, no. 69 (March 1972), pp. 61-73.
2 Lyster-Denny, *Memorial*, p. 43.
3 NLI, Moran Papers, Ms. 1544, p. 157.
4 NLI, Freeholders County Roscommon 1768-99, Ms. 10130.
5 Lyster-Denny, *Memorial*, p. 37.
6 RD, Deed No. 519-361-340403.
7 NA, Landed estates court rentals, vol. 56, no. 10, p. 17.
8 RD, Deed No. 156-228-104533.
9 RD, Deed No. 555-58-367231.
10 Lyster-Denny, *Memorial*, p. 55.
11 NA, Valuation Office Field Books, OL 4.1590.
12 NA, Religious census of the diocese of Elphin, M 2466.
13 Lyster-Denny, *Memorial*, p. 109.
14 Lyster-Denny, *Memorial*, p. 24.
15 NLI, Moran Papers, Ms 1544 p. 147.
16 Lyster-Denny, *Memorial*, p. 112.
17 RD, Deed No. 394-37-259435.
18 RD, Deed No. 394-37-259435.
19 RD, Deed No. 398-56-262326.
20 NA, Chancery Decree, RC, 6/6, p. 43.
21 RD, Deed No. 689-519-473854.
22 N.A., Religious census of the diocese of Elphin, M 2466.
23 RD, Deed No. 164-239-110386.
24 RD, Deed No. 191-273-127971.
25 RD, Deed No. 240-63-153378.
26 RD, Deed No. 698-139-478870.
27 RD, Deed No. 422-454-276781.
28 Arthur Moore, 'The McKeoghs of Moyfinn, Part 2' in *Journal of the Old Athlone Society*, ii, no. 5 (1978), p. 62.
29 RD, Deed No. 274-481-180657.
30 RD, Deed No. 287-1-184559.
31 RD, Deed No. 673-88-463044.
32 RD, Deed No. 1852; 10-283-269.
33 RD, Deed No. 129-118-86443
34 RD, Deed No. 160-444-102994.
35 RD, Deed No. 283-495-185753.
36 NLI, Moran Papers, Ms 1544, p. 276.
37 Eileen O'Byrne, *The convert rolls* (Dublin, 1981), p. 95.
38 O'Byrne, *The convert rolls*, p. 170.
39 Genealogical Office, I.G.R.S. Collection 103, tombstone No. 8.
40 RD, Deed No. 466-416-298192.

41 RD, Deed No. 453-443-292083.
42 RD, Deed NO. 460-393-294681.
43 RD, Deed No. 287-79-185075.
44 RD, Deed No. 630-532-438323.
45 RD, Deed No. 821-363-55898
46 NA, Tithe applotment book, Cam parish, Tab 25/51 No. 14.
47 RD, Deed No. 783-177-529912.
48 NA, Landed estates court rentals, Vol 6, No. 53 Plots 5 and 6.
49 RD, Deed No. 563-522-380435.
50 NA, Landed estates court rentals, Vol. 60 No. 33.
51 RD, Deed No. 598-396-410548.
52 RD, Deed No. 598-403-410568.
53 Roman Catholic parish register, Kiltoom & Cam parish, Elphin diocese, (in local custody)
54 William Gacquin, *Tombstone inscriptions Cam old cemetery* (1992), p. 25.
55 RD, Deed No. 633-99-432418.
56 William Gacquin, *Tombstone inscriptions Cam old cemetery* (1992), p. 25.
57 RD, Deed No. 878-272-582773.
58 Bermingham, *Home colonies*, pp. 140-149.
59 NA, Tithe applotment book, Cam parish, Tab 25/51.
60 Church of Ireland, vestry minutes, Kiltoom parish, Typescript copy, Burgess Papers, Athlone Library, p. 53.
61 Church of Ireland, marriage register, Kiltoom parish, Typescript copy, Burgess Papers, Athlone Library, p. 73.
62 Roman Catholic, parish register, Kiltoom and Cam parish. Elphin diocese (in local custody).
63 NLI, Freeholders List, county Roscommon, 1768-69, Ms. 10130.
64 NLI, Freeholders List, county Roscommon, 1795-96, Ms. 10130.
65 NA, Landed estates court rentals, Vol. 60 No. 33.
66 NLI, Freeholders List, county Roscommon, 1813-1818.
67 O'Byrne, *The convert rolls*, p. 95
68 NLI, Freeholders List, county Roscommon, 1836-1844.
69 RD, Deed No. 1848-4-57-93.
70 RD, Deed No. 673-88-463044.
71 Map of county Roscommon showing the several properties of the county in 1852-3, Reproduced in *Rosc Chomain 1973*, C.B.S. Magazine (Roscommon, 1973)
72 Irish Land Commission, Record No. LC2363, Box 1539.
73 Church of Ireland, Vestry minutes, Kiltoom parish, Typescript copy, Burgess papers, Athlone Library, p. 26.

THE IMPROVING LANDLORDS

1 R.C.Simington, 'The tithe applotment books of 1834', in *Dept. of Agriculture Journal*, xxxviii, no. 2 (1941), p. 242.
2 NA, Tithe applotment book, Kiltoom Parish, Tab 25/52.
3 Church of Ireland, vestry minutes, Kiltoom Parish, Burgess Papers, Athlone Library, p. 32.
4 NA, Tithe applotment book, Cam Parish, Tab 25/51.
5 Church of Ireland Vestry Minutes, Kiltoom Parish, Burgess Papers, Athlone Library, p. 33.
6 Simington, 'Tithe applotment books of 1834', p. 243.
7 *The census of Ireland for the year 1851*, Pt. I, [1550] H.C. 1852-3 xcii 515, pp. 517-18 and 520-21.
8 NLI, Moran Papers, Ms. 1544, p. 367.
9 Marcus MacEnry, 'Memoirs of Brian Ó Fearghail' in *Eigse* v (1945-47), p. 159.
10 NLI, Moran Papers, Ms. 1544, p. 635.
11 Church of Ireland, vestry minutes, Burgess Papers, Athlone Library, p. iii.
12 RD, Deed No. 766-343-519878.
13 NA, National Schools Applications, County Roscommon, ED 1 76/3.
14 Church of Ireland, Parish Register Kiltoom Parish, Burgess Papers, Athlone Library, p. 60.
15 *Fourth report of the commissioners on the bogs of Ireland*, April 1814, H.C. 1829, iv, p. 601.
16 *Fourth report on bogs*, p. 601.
17 *Fourth report on bogs*, p. 602.
18 *Fourth report on bogs*, p. 603.
19 *Fourth report on bogs*, p. 601.
20 *Fourth report on bogs*, p. 603.
21 *Fourth report on bogs*, p. 601.
22 *Fourth report on bogs*, p. 603.
23 *Fourth report on bogs*, p. 602.

24 NLI, Moran Papers, Ms 1544, p. 147.

25 *Fourth report on bogs*, p. 609.

26 *Fourth report on bogs*, p. 622.

27 NA, Tithe applotment books, Kiltoom Parish, Tab 25/52 p. 13.

28 *The census of Ireland 1851*, Pt.1 [1150] H.C. 1852-3, xcii.515, p. 521.

29 *Fourth report on bogs*, p. 609.

30 Thomas Bermingham, *Home colonies*, p. 143.

31 Timothy Cronin, 'The foundations of landlordism in the Barony of Athlone 1566-1666', M.A. Thesis U.C.G. 1977, pp. 69-70.

32 N.A., Tithe applotment book, Cam Parish, Tab 25/51, p. 20.

33 Bermingham, *Home colonies*, p. 141.

34 Bermingham, *Home colonies*, p. 141.

35 Bermingham, *Home colonies*, p. 140.

36 Bermingham, *Home colonies*, p. 140.

37 Bermingham, *Home colonies*, p. 147.

38 Bermingham, *Home colonies*, p. 142.

39 Bermingham, *Home colonies*, p. 142.

40 Bermingham, *Home colonies*, p. 144.

41 Bermingham, *Home colonies*, p. 142.

42 Bermingham, *Home colonies*, p. 147.

43 Bermingham, *Home colonies*, p. 144.

44 Bermingham, *Home colonies*, p. 145.

45 Bermingham, *Home colonies*, p. 144.

46 NLI, Moran Papers, Ms 1544, p. 495.

47 Vera Hughes, *The strange story of Sarah Kelly* (Moate, 1988), pp. 64-5.

48 *The census of Ireland 1851*, Pt. 1, [1150], H.C. 1852-3 xii.515, p. 518.

A TIME OF CHANGE

1 *Returns of population of several counties of Ireland as enumerated in 1831*, H.C. 1833 (254) xxxix. 1 p. 42; and *The census of Ireland for the year 1851* [1550] H.C. 1852-3, xcii.515 pp. 517-18 and 520-1.

2 K.H. Connell, *The population of Ireland 1750-1845* (Oxford, 1950), pp. 2-3.

3 R.M. Harris, D.M. Jacobes (eds.), *The search for missing friends, vol. 1 1831-50* (Boston, 1989), p. 139.

4 *Census of Ireland 1861 part IV* H.C.1863 [3204-111] lx.1 vol. II, pp. 172-3.

5 *First Report of the Royal Commission on the state of Religious and other Public Instruction in Ireland* H.C.1835 xxxiii.1,829 Appendix p. 774.

6 Griffiths Valuation, County Roscommon, barony of Athlone, 1855.

7 *Abstract of Returns persuant to an Act for taking account of population in Great Britain* H.C. 1843,[497] xxiv. p. 526.

8 Bermingham, *Home colonies*, p. 147.

9 Lyster-Denny, *Memorial*, p. 30.

10 RD, Deed No. 460-393-294681.

11 Vera Hughes, *The strange story of Sarah Kelly* (Moate, 1988) pp. 24-6.

12 Gearoid O Tuathaigh, *Ireland before the famine 1798-1848* (Dublin, 1972), p. 98.

13 *Second Report of the Commissioners of Irish Education Inquiry*, H.C. 1826, vol. xii, p. 1282.

14 *Second Report of the Commissioners of Irish Education Inquiry*, H.C. 1826, vol. xii 1, p. 1284.

15 *First Report of the Royal Commission on the state of Religious and other Public Instruction in Ireland*, H.C.1835, xxxiii, Appendix p. 774.

16 *Second Report of the Commission on the state of Religious and other Public Instruction in Ireland*, H.C. 1835, xxxiv, pp. 785-86.

17 NLI, Moran Papers, Ms. 1544, pp. 370-71.

18 O'Tuathaigh, *Ireland before the famine*, p. 101.

19 NA, National school applications, county Roscommon, ED 1 76/3.

20 NA, National school applications, county Roscommon, ED 1 76/8.

21 NA, Register of national schools, county Roscommon, ED 2 39/9.

22 NA, National school applications, county Roscommon, ED 1 76/11.

23 NA, National schools applications, county Roscommon, ED 1 76/12.

24 NA, Register of national schools, county Roscommon, ED 2 39/15

25 NA, Register of national schools, county Roscommon, ED 2 39/15.

26 NA, Register of national schools, county Roscommon, ED 2 39/68.

27 NA, Register of national schools, county Roscommon, ED 2 39/24.

28 NA, Register of national schools,

county Roscommon, ED 2 39/11.

29 NA, Register of national schools,
county Roscommon, ED 2 39/11.

30 NA, National school applications,
county Roscommon, ED 1 76/3.

31 NA, Register of national schools,
county Roscommon, ED 2 39/64.

32 NA, Register of national schools,
county Roscommon. ED 2 39/64

33 Stone plaque on church wall at
Curraghboy with Fr O'Neill's name
and the date 1830.

34 Roman Catholic parish register,
Kiltoom & Cam parish, Elphin diocese,
(in local custody).

35 NLI, Moran Papers, Ms 1544, p. 416.

36 NLI, Moran Papers, Ms 1544, pp. 374-
75.

37 Roman Catholic Parish Register,
Kiltoom & Cam Parish, Elphin
Diocese, (local custody).

38 O.S. County Roscommon, Sheet 49,
first edition 1837.

39 Samuel Lewis, *Topographical dictionary of
Ireland*, ii, p. 215.

40 Lewis, *Topographical dictionary of Ireland*,
i, p. 244.

41 Church of Ireland, Vestry minutes,
Kiltoom Parish, Burgess Papers,
Athlone Library, p. 6.

42 Church of Ireland, Vestry minutes,
Kiltoom Parish, Burgess Papers,
Athlone Library, p. 9.

43 NA, Religious Census of diocese of
Elphin 1749, M 2466.

44 Lyster-Denny, *Memorial*, p. 30.

45 Lyster-Denny, *Memorial*, p. 24.

46 Lyster-Denny, *Memorial*, p. 25.

47 NLI, Moran Papers, Ms 1544, p. 420.

48 NLI, Moran Papers, Ms 1544, p. 443.

49 NA, State of the country papers,
county Roscommon, 1408/38

50 NLI, Moran Papers, Ms 1544, pp. 232-
3.

51 NLI, Moran Papers, Ms 1544, p. 90.

52 NLI, Moran Papers, Ms 1544, p. 208.

53 NA, Outrage Papers, county
Roscommon, 1847, 25/122.

54 NA, Outrage Papers, county
Roscommon, 1835.

55 NLI, Moran Papers, Ms 1544, p. 11.

56 NLI, Moran Papers, Ms 1544, p. 31.

57 NLI, Moran Papers, Ms 1544, p. 61.

58 Church of Ireland, parish register,
Kiltoom parish,Burgess Papers, Athlone
Library, p. 61.

59 N.A., Board of Cholera Papers, county
Roscommon, 1832-34, 2/440/9.

60 NLI, Moran Papers, Ms 1544, p. 314.

61 *First report of the commission of inquiry into
the state of the poorer classes in Ireland*,
H.C. 1835 xxxii part 2, Appendix A,
p. 6.

62 Issac Weld, *Statistical survey of the county
Roscommon* (Dublin, 1832), p. 504.

63 *First report of the commission of poor
inquiry*, Appendix A, p. 843.

64 Church of Ireland, parish register,
Kiltoom parish, Burgess Papers,
Athlone Library, p. 65.

65 Church of Ireland, parish register,
Kiltoom parish, Burgess Papers,
Athlone Library, p. 73.

66 *First report of poor inquiry*, Appendix B, p
108.

67 *Commission of inquiry into the state of the
law and practice in respect to occupation of
land in Ireland* (Devon Commission)
Minutes of evidence, Pt. 11, H.C. 1845
[616] xx.1, p. 342.

68 Devon Commission, minutes of evidence, Pt 11, p. 344.

69 Devon Commission, Minutes of evidence, Pt 111, H.C. 1845 [657] xxi.1,
pp. 922-4.

70 Valuations Office, Ely Place, Dublin,
Field Book, parish of Cam. county
Roscommon.

71 Devon Commission, minutes of
evidence, Pt. 111, p. 922.

72 Devon Commission, minutes of
evidence, Pt. 11, p. 336.

73 Devon Commission, minutes of
evidence, Pt. 111, p. 923.

74 Devon Commission, minuets of
evidence, Pt. 11, p. 344.

75 Devon Commission, minutes of
evidence, Pt. 111, p. 922.

76 Devon Commission, minutes of
evidence, Pt. 11, p. 344.

77 Devon Commission, minutes of
evidence, Pt. 11, p. 336.

78 Devon Commission, minutes of
evidence, Pt. 111, p. 923.

79 Devon Commission, minutes of
    evidence, Pt 11, p. 336.
80 O'Tuathaigh, *Ireland before the famine*,
    p. 113.
81 NA, Relief commission Papers 11, 2,
    2/441/46.
82 *The census of Ireland for the year 1851*, p.
    518.
83 Lyster-Denny, *Memorial*, p. 25.
84 *Relief of Distress papers, Athlone
    Union, 1848*, H.C. 1847-48, lvi, pp.
    890-900.

85 Roman Catholic parish register,
    Kiltoom & Cam parish, Elphin
    Diocese (local custody).
86 Griffith's Valuation, county
    Roscommon, barony of Athlone.
87 'Report on the state of popery in
    Ireland 1731' in *Archivium Hibernicium*,
    iii (1914), p. 140.
88 Lewis, *Topographical dictionary of Ireland*,
    I, p.244.
89 *Parliamentry Gazetter of Ireland*, (2 vols,
    Dublin, 1844), i, p. 279.